Modern Urban Landscapes

Creating Energy-Efficient Designs

Modern Urban Landscapes

Edited by Martin Coyle

Creating Energy-Efficient Designs

images
Publishing

Preface

The modern city is a series of interconnecting and interrelated spaces that require an energy-efficient urban landscape. These are sites that transcend their primary function as public or private spaces, with a secondary and sometimes even tertiary function such as stormwater storage or flood mitigation. This energy-efficient urban landscape must be robust, innovative, and functional but also maintain its primary function as places for people. Landscape architects, architects, and engineers have all worked in collaboration with local governments, developers, and suppliers to closely analyse how infrastructure works in the modern city. Now these pieces of green infrastructure are being assembled, by talented and multi-disciplinary teams, into energy-efficient urban landscapes around the world, improving the local micro- and macroclimates to make our modern cities better places to live.

Since the Industrial Revolution began in the 1760s, modern society has revolved around city life. With an unprecedented wave of urbanisation across the world, for the first time ever most populations are now highly urbanised, leading to increased demands on the environment through direct and indirect means. Our modern cities are increasingly facing challenges such as high energy consumption; air, water and noise pollution; and a decrease in quality of life. These increased demands on the city environment are now slowly being turned around through the progressive, piece-by-piece installation of energy-efficient urban landscapes, which first improve their local environment, and then begin to reshape the city as a whole.

Rapid urbanisation in cities has led to increasing amounts of nonporous paving, which has increased stormwater runoff, created more frequent or more severe flood events, reduced aquifer recharging, and worsened water pollution. Traditional 'pipe and pit' systems concentrate on the rapid removal of stormwater from the system, leading to flooding and the loss of a precious resource before it can be reused.

Through engagement with local and state governments, designers, landscape architects, and engineers alike have pioneered the use of water-sensitive urban design, managing the life cycle of urban water, and putting in place systems for capturing, detaining, and treating urban stormwater to improve its quality, store for reuse, and detain to prevent flood events.

Energy-efficient urban landscapes manage urban stormwater in a variety of ways. Bioretention processes, such as tree pits, swales, and basins, and porous paving can retain and remove pollutants from the stormwater, while retaining water to mitigate floods. Both porous paving and bioretention can also act to recharge groundwater aquifers, the source of drinking water for many cities. Additionally, bioretention systems remove nitrogen and phosphorous from the water cycle, the by-products of modern fertiliser runoff and the source of dangerous algal blooms that de-oxygenate water courses and interfere with the aquatic life cycle. Through engagement with local authorities, developers, and designers, water-sensitive urban design can progressively improve the quality of urban runoff to rivers and oceans, improving water management cycles within our modern cities.

More and more buildings are being designed with green roofs and green walls, for multiple reasons. As part of the overall stormwater cycle, green roofs are able to detain, filter, and slowly release stormwater, preventing flood events. An additional benefit of both systems is the insulation that green-roof systems and walls can provide, cutting down on the solar radiation to which the building is exposed and therefore reducing the cooling/heating costs. Not only do these systems provide water quality and insulation, but they can also add value to developments by providing private or public open spaces. Some European cities have a residential and municipal requirement for a roof space of more than 1076 square feet (100 square meters) to be a green roof. Aesthetically, internal and external green walls, through the patronage of designers such as Patrick Le Blanc, have become accepted as good design and necessary in the scheme of the city.

As many cities face water-supply issues, energy-efficient urban landscapes can aid irrigation and retention of habitat through water harvesting and greywater reuse. Reed bed and sand filters have been used for millennia, with mentions in Sanskrit and Egyptian writings from before 400 BC. The reuse of water in urban areas has gradually been gaining prominence due to the scarcity of this precious resource in many Western and Middle Eastern countries, including Australia. Filtration through residential reed bed and sand filters has become increasingly promoted for off-system sewer systems. It also enables relatively 'clean' water to be reused in gardens, reducing potable-water consumption. Treating sewer-grade waste is still carefully managed, but alternative residential wastewater is a valuable garden resource in many countries, and should be integrated as often as possible.

Reducing energy consumption is one of the key parameters to energy-efficient urban landscapes. Simple age-old measures such as good site design can create a favourable micro- and macroclimate. Where green roofs and walls can provide direct thermal insulation to buildings, well-planned and designed, appropriately specified street trees can also vastly improve the microclimate for a building, a street, or an entire precinct. Another age-old technique is making the most of shade in extreme climates to negate the extent of electricity required to cool buildings and public spaces. When streetscape and shade-tree plantings become combined with integrated rainwater harvesting and bioretention, the benefits of an energy-efficient urban landscape quickly become obvious, and a matter of 'Why didn't we always do this?'.

When the sun goes down, reducing energy consumption is also a priority. Over the last 10 years, LED technology has improved, becoming vastly more cost-effective. High-pressure sodium (HPS) streetlights used in many countries consume a lot of energy, and as a result, many local governments and state agencies have been quietly and conservatively trialling LED street lights. Some cities, such as Los Angeles, have commenced wide-scale replacement programs, and have recorded energy savings of up to 40 percent per annum as a result of replacing HPS lights with LED lights. The benefits of LEDs are two-fold: reduced consumption and extended life, leading to lower capital costs. HPS streetlights are historically rated to run for about 20,000 hours, where as LED technology is now being conservatively rated to run for more than 50,000 hours, almost doubling the life of the fixture and inherent replacement costs. These hours can be extended even more if coupled with advanced sensor lighting in areas where constant lighting is not required, such as occasional usage places.

As designers of modern urban environments, landscape architects and engineers work to create energy-efficient urban landscapes that combine aesthetics with function in a manner never seen before. Innovative techniques and technologies, as showcased in this book, allow our cities and landscapes to work in unison with nature, creating modern forms that benefit from timeless cycles of light, shade, and rain. As energy-efficient urban landscape techniques are adopted first by individual developments, then at the precinct scale, suburb by suburb, they will transform and rejuvenate the cities in which we live, and ultimately improve all of our lives.

Martin Coyle

Contents

5 Rainwater Recycling and other Rainwater Management Technologies

6 Soil Improving and Intelligent Water-saving Technologies

7 Low-maintenance Technology

Urban Landscaping and Energy Consumption

'Landscape' seems a simple word, but is a beautiful and obscure concept. It is defined in Webster's dictionary as 'a picture that shows a natural scene of land or the countryside'. In fact, there are varied understandings of it in different disciplines. For example, a geographer may define 'landscape' scientifically, understanding it as a terrain scene or a comprehensive natural geographic area, or a generic term for a certain type of scene such as city landscape and forest landscape. An artist would understand it as a subject of presentation and representation, or perhaps scenery. But an architect will comprehend it as the background of buildings. An ecologist may read it as an ecosystem. Many supporters of city-beautification campaigns and city developers equate the landscape to urban street facades, neon lights, plants, and garden features. The 'landscape' we are going to explore in this book refers to city landscape. It consists of all kinds of interactive visual substances and visual events that exist in the urban environment, including a rich variety of contents, such as buildings, bridges, roads, plazas, greenbelts, water features, garden features, and sculptures.

All these elements of city landscape provide a large quantity of materials for creating high-quality urban spaces; therefore, the creation of urban landscape has always played an important role in city development schedules around the world. Particularly as nations are attaching increasing importance to environmental issues, city landscape becomes an infrastructure for creating a sustainable urban ecological environment and brings about remarkable ecological, social, and economic effects. However, with increasing parks, plazas, water features, and greenbelts as well as improved urban ecological environments, we have to confront another question: energy consumption of landscaping.

Compared with energy consumption of a single large building, that of a single landscape may be minimal; yet together, these can add up to a large amount of energy consumption. Not to mention the huge cost of labor, electricity, and water necessary for the normal operation of a big-city garden or a fountain plaza; the maintenance fee of urban greenbelts alone can make some cities with scarce water resources feel financial strains. Take China for instance. According to the authorities, China's urban greenbelts will have a demand for water as high as about 292 billion cubic feet (8.27 billion cubic meters) by 2030. Such a huge amount obviously reveals the severe demand of energy consumption of landscaping.

For these reasons, more and more landscape designers are beginning to integrate low-energy consumption technologies such as remote-sensing, system-based automatic irrigation technology; intelligent illumination; and rainwater management technology into their designs. These designs have not only greatly reduced energy consumption of landscaping, but have also improved sustainability of urban ecological environments. This book categorizes these technologies into seven types:

1. remote-sensing, system-based automatic irrigation technology

2. intelligent illumination and intelligent lighting technology

3. wind-power technology

4. solar photovoltaic power generation technology

5. rainwater recycling and other rainwater management technologies

6. soil-improving and intelligent water-saving technologies

7. low-maintenance technology.

The following text introduces these seven types of technologies, and illustrates them with excellent design cases, aiming to provide inspiration to designers of lower-energy landscaping.

1 | Remote-sensing, System-based Automatic Irrigation Technology

Water-remote-sensing technology

Vegetation water-remote-sensing technology can be used to monitor water contents of landscapes and timely transmit information. In this way, it can be adopted to protect landscaping resources or monitor water contents of large areas of urban greenbelts and present, in data, the irrigation time.

Remote-sensing monitoring and sensing positioning are a major part of intellectualization. They play a key role in lowering energy consumption of landscaping. They are applied in the following three aspects in landscaping projects: FDR system (sensing system technology), FDR collection system (data collection system), and remote management software (data management and analysis). The three parts constitute the whole process.

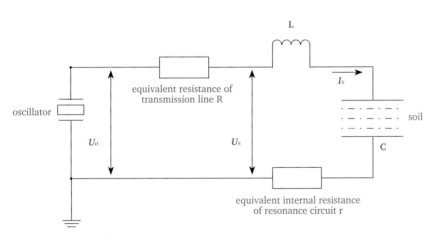

Diagram 1: Assistant resonant circuit under high frequency

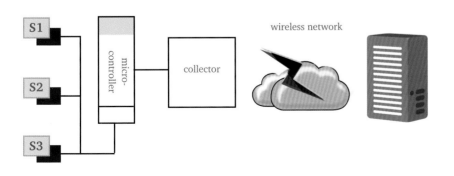

Diagram 2: Structure of collection system

FDR system (sensing system technology)

When FDR (frequency domain reflection) technology is applied, a certain range of frequency scanning test signals will be sent. Wherever the signals come into different conductor resistance, stronger reflection signals with the same frequency but at different time periods will be produced. These feedback signals will be analyzed through Fourier conversion methods, and the distance to the route barriers will be calculated by measuring the peak frequency of reflection signals. (see diagram 1)

FDR collection system (data collection system)

The landscape's data measures water content of landscaping greenbelt; therefore, the FDR-based water collection system of landscaping vegetation soil has multiple sensors installed at varied depths. The structure of water collection system is shown in diagram 2.

Sensors S1, S2 and S3 are connected to micro-controllers by homogeneous transmission lines, while the micro-controllers poll all sensor resonance circuits and acquire test data that will be further processed by the collectors. To facilitate the installation of measuring instruments in the field and to send timely data to the server, the system adopts a wireless communication system and sends standardized data packages to a central data server through public mobile communication networks.

Remote management software (data management and analysis)

Remote management software installed in the central server can remotely control the sensing collectors for vegetation soil water and process the collected data. It can also manage several detectors and collectors for vegetation soil water and form a vegetation water-detection network.

The software has four major functions: parameter setting, data conversion, data display, and data transmission. As the collectors control FDR sensors at multiple layers and each sensor is located at varied depths and is in contact with different parts of vegetation, the system can, by setting parameters, save the data concerning depths of each installed sensor and physical constants of vegetation soil touched by the sensors. Finally, the system can get water contents of soil by collecting and analyzing the data, which can be used as important parameters for maintaining landscaping vegetation.

Automatic irrigation system

The demand for green environments has been increasing along with the rapid growth of global economy and enhancement of living standards. Drip-irrigation technology plays an important role in saving water resources and creating a green environment. Its water droppers can slowly drip water under low pressure, providing filtrated water, fertilizer, and other chemicals for the soil. The application of drip-irrigation technology in landscaping designs can sharply enhance usage ratio of water, reduce destruction to soil structure, and improve the ecological environment and economic efficiency. It is new efficient, water-saving irrigation technology. In landscaping designs, it is a significant water-resource-management development that can help achieve highly efficient and accurate irrigation.

Wireless, auto-control, water-saving, drip-irrigation systems can offer timely and accurate drip irrigation. This system takes advantage of the ad-hoc ZigBee wireless sensor network, and uses a star network of topological structure. It can monitor changes of soil temperature and humidity of landscape in different locations. By giving feedback of sensing signals, it can determine and control dripping actions.

The ZigBee wireless network is characterized by low cost, low-power consumption, low speed, close distance, short time delay, high safety standards, etc. It can communicate with the network coordinator nodes of development platforms according to the plants' demand for water in different growth periods and based on soil humidity and environmental temperature. Thus, the landscape controller can accurately and scientifically control the location, time, water volume, and quality of irrigation, and realize automatic drip irrigation of plants and provide excellent growth conditions for landscaping vegetation. The system offers a basis for unified dispatching management of large landscape and is an ideal solution to water-saving irrigation.

The automatic drip system uses the star network topological structure, which is an irregular network of wireless sensors. Its overall structure is shown in diagram 3 and consists of an upper computer, network coordinator nodes, wireless transceiver modules (ZigBee communication module), terminal control nodes, and actuators.

The system uses an upper computer to receive, store, and analyze the data uploaded from sensors, and control the best options for drip irrigation.

Network coordinator nodes, as coordinators for the whole network, are responsible for automatically searching terminal nodes in the network, organizing wireless network, collecting needed data from terminal nodes, and facilitating communications between terminal nodes and the upper computer. The network coordinator nodes and terminal control nodes form a network and communicate with each other through ZigBee-based wireless transceiver modules. The transceiver module is composed of a host computer module for the use of a network coordinator and several slave computer terminal modules. The terminal control node is based on site controllers, while the field controller (1) is fixed to the main pipe and equipped with a liquid level sensor, a pressure sensor, and a flow sensor. The actuator is a frequency changer for adjusting pressure. The field controller (2) to field controller (n) are exactly the same and are distributed in every landscaping area. They are also equipped with soil humidity and temperature sensors. A terminal node module can be connected with several probes for temperature and humidity when necessary, while the actuator is an electromagnetic valve for controlling the starting and closing of the drip-irrigation system.

Besides, with a view to the decentralizing character and cost of landscaping, a solar photovoltaic power supply system could be used to supply power for terminal control nodes.

Soil humidity is an important variable of an automatic drip-irrigation system. The upper computer sends wireless orders for collection to the site controllers, receives and displays feedback data from the sensors, ranks humidity values, judges whether the liquid level is proper, combines the data from pressure and flow sensors to adjust the frequency changer, and finally gives commands through ZigBee communication boards to the site controller to open or close the electromagnetic valve.

When the sensor nodes are supplied with power, the system is initialized, and then the nodes choose a communication channel and join the existing ZigBee wireless network, and finally hibernate to wait for receiving signals. When the sensor nodes receive inquiring signals from the gateway node, they start to collect data and send it to the coordinator node.

Upon receiving commands for collection from the upper computer, the site controller will begin to gather and upload data on soil humidity, air temperature, liquid level, pressure, flow,

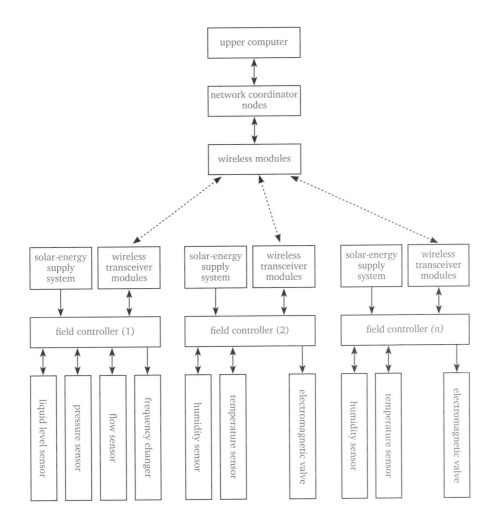

Diagram 3: Structure of the automatic drip system

etc. It then waits for the upper computer to issue commands to open and close electromagnetic valves, and adjust frequency changers, which the site controller will execute.

The site controllers of wireless water-saving automatic drip-irrigation control systems can monitor soil humidity and environmental temperature of plants in real time, and send sensor signals to the control center through wireless transceiver modules. The control center can accurately receive information about the work status of the current system in real time, and activate the automatic drip system so as to save water for landscaping. Any communication outage or abnormal water pressure will be immediately sent back to the control center, which will notify relative staff to carry out maintenance by voice alarms or other means, and thus improve the reliability of the whole system. This system uses ZigBee technology and has a simple network structure. The arrangement of the landscaping site is very flexible. Therefore, the automatic irrigation system is much more practical and is more efficient in its use of water. It

can save labor and expenses for wiring and piping, dispense with manual operation, as well as work steadily for a long time. It can facilitate installation, maintenance, and recycling of the system for big areas, providing a power tool for landscaping project designs and maintenance.

Shapoorji Pallonji Infocity

A 80-acre (32-hectare) multi-use complex, Shapoorji Pallonji Infocity is dominated by the circular arterial road. A slightly recessed entry to the property leads to this circular road with a 1-acre (4050-square-meter) front garden comprising a large pond, a mist fountain, and lawns. The circular arterial road is joined further ahead by linking roads in a segmental arc formation. The resulting road pattern takes care of the vehicular traffic on the periphery, leaving the central, lush, landscaped spaces for pedestrians. At present, the complex consists of office blocks (mainly occupied by renowned IT business houses), a clubhouse, a park, and a small residential area.

Within the office building complex, the central plaza plays a major role. With meandering pedestrian walks leading to the central paved area, this space is where the hard-working IT professionals can de-stress and indulge in social networking. Four fountain basins and circular flower beds underscore the central axis, around which three curvilinear IT blocks are symmetrically placed and lead the eye to a water cascade, which acts as the focal point, with the clubhouse as a backdrop.

The clubhouse, amphitheater, and a swimming pool are placed firmly on the central north–south axis. The park has a large party lawn, pedestrian paths, and jogging track, which act as a buffer between the IT blocks and the clubhouse. The parking lots provided on either side, conveniently tucked within trees, are shrouded with greenery at the same time.

This office block has a large basement with parking facilities. The roof of the basement offers an opportunity to create a large, 2-acre (8100-square-meter) garden, overlooked by three office blocks. Here, a service block of an electric substation juts out above the garden level, which is converted into the focal point for the entire landscape, laid in a formal pattern.

Trees form a major component of the campus greenery. They provide the environmental benefit of creating a cool, dust-free microclimate. All the greenery is sustained by an automatic irrigation system fed by the recycled water from the sewage treatment plant, which ensures that, irrespective of monsoon rainfall, the landscape will remain lush throughout the year.

Location |
Pune, India
Completion date |
2012
Site area |
80 acres (32.4 hectares)
Landscape design |
Kishore D Pradhan
Client |
Manjri Stud Farm, a subsidiary of M/s
Shapoorji Pallonji & Co. Ltd
Photography |
Kishore D Pradhan and SP Infocity

1. Central plaza
2. Podium landscape
3. Pathway leading to central plaza

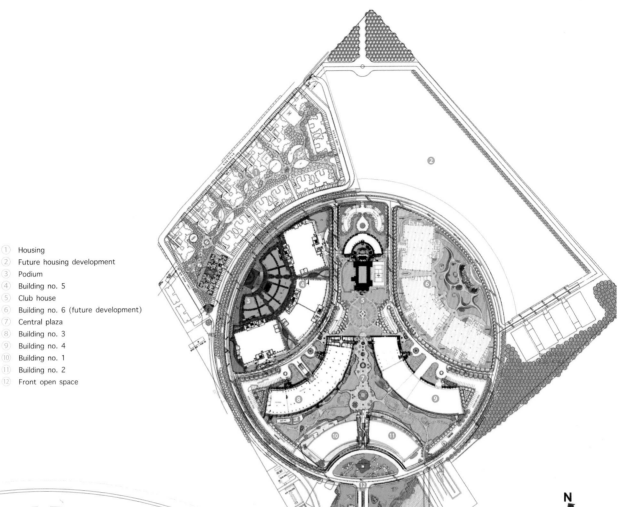

1 Housing
2 Future housing development
3 Podium
4 Building no. 5
5 Club house
6 Building no. 6 (future development)
7 Central plaza
8 Building no. 3
9 Building no. 4
10 Building no. 1
11 Building no. 2
12 Front open space

Master plan

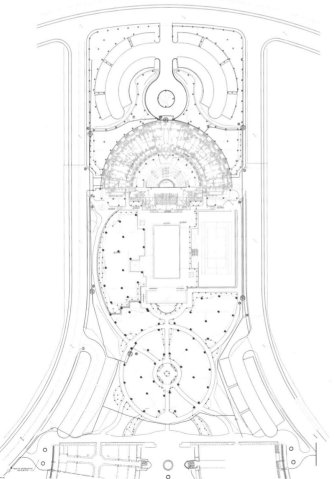

Irrigation layout

———————— pipe, 3.5 inches (90 mm); 6 kg per square centimeter

———————— pipe, 2.5 inches (63 mm); 6 kg per square centimeter

● Maxi paw sprinkler

• Uni spray pop up sprinkler

——————— LLDPE tubing, 0.8 inches (20 mm)

——————— tubing, 0.6 inches (16 mm)

✳ Micro sprinklers

⊗ Ball valve, 2.5 inches (63 mm)

⊗ Ball valve, 3.5 inches (90 mm)

⊙ Air-release, 2.5 inches (63 mm)

⊙ Pressure-release, 2.5 inches (63 mm)

○ Water source / Tank

1 | 2 | 3 | 4

① Coping in 1.97 inches (50 millimeters) of polished granite with 0.98-inch (25-millimeters) bull nosing edge
② Cladding in flamed multicolor granite
③ Cladding in polished multicolor granite
④ Paving in red Agra red granite 1.18 inches (30 millimeters)
⑤ 0.79-inch (20-millimeter) screed
⑥ Brick filling

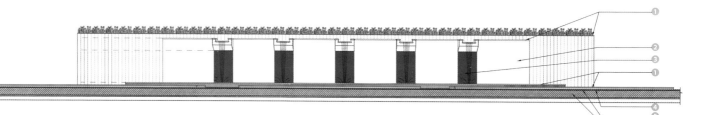

Front Elevation

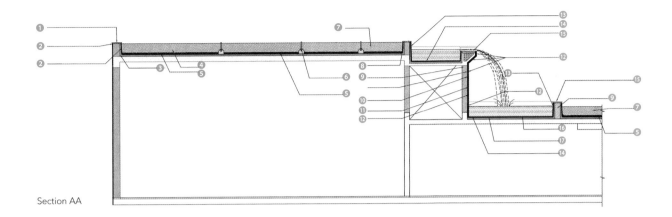

Section AA

① Coping in 1.97 inches (50 millimeters) of polished Kotah with 0.98-inch (25-millimeter) bull nosing edge
② 0.79-inch (20-millimeter) plaster
③ 2.76 inches (75 millimeters) of waterproofing layer laid to slope
④ Earth fill
⑤ 2.76 inches (75 millimeters) of drainage layer
⑥ 1.97 inches (50 millimeters) of shahbad tile edging as per shrubbery pattern
⑦ Earth fill
⑧ 2.76 inches (75 millimeters) of waterproofing layer
⑨ 9.06 inches (230 millimeters) of brick wall
⑩ Waterproofing liner
⑪ 0.79-inch (20-millimeter) screed
⑫ Cladding in polished multicolor granite
⑬ Finish in Italia tiles (Algae)
⑭ Finish in Italia tiles (Algae BC)
⑮ Cladding in polished multicolor granite
⑯ Water-body liner
⑰ 0.79 inches (20 millimeters) of cement screed

1. Landscape at the *Entrance*
2. Fountain in *Central* plaza
3. Drip Irrigation *System for Mass Tree Planting*
4. Mist fountain framed by road side silver oak trees

Energy Complex, ENCO

The new complex was developed on a site that is flanked by two major arterial streets and located within 1640.4 feet (500 meters) of the junction of sky train and underground mass transit. The 11.5-acre (4.6-hectare) site, with a total 7.4 acres (3 hectares) of rental space, comprises three buildings. Architects, landscape architects, and the client had worked closely to find the optimum solution to utilize the site, a devastated land of Railroad Authority. Three-dimensional computer models were used as tools to study the building mass and its microclimate for outdoor spaces, in order to select the appropriate location for the project.

Wind-tunnel testing, and shade and shadow study also helped to confirm the location of trees and recreation zone for people. Under LEED criteria for water-resource management, rainwater from the buildings and the plaza were collected in underground tanks for irrigation. Water-moisture sensor technology was introduced to help control the irrigation system for the whole complex. The building roofs are equipped with solar panels to harvest the solar energy during the day, which is used for garden lighting at night. Facilities such as bike trails from the mass-transit station and bus station, bicycle parking, and shower facilities are provided to encourage the use of bicycles as alternative transportation.

The project is conceptualized as a sustainable and environmentally friendly building. The planning and design used the 'Greenovative' ideas in implementing the cutting-edge technology as tools for energy saving. This is a pilot project to encourage public and private agencies to use energy in a more efficient ways.

Every detail of ENCO was designed to meet international standards. It is the first building complex in Thailand and Southeast Asia that has been certified as meeting LEED standards.

Location |
Bangkok, Thailand

Completion date |
2010

Site area |
12 acres (4.8 hectares)

Landscape design |
Axis Landscape Company Limited

Client |
Energy Complex Co. Ltd

Photography |
Anawat Pedsuwan, Niphon Fahkrachang, Aukkalayot Petch-um-pai, Boonpin Thuethong, Wanniwat Ussawathanaphaisarn, Wiratchai Wansamngarm

Award |
LEED Platinum certification from Green Building Council, United States in 2010

1. Drop-off at arrival plaza
2. View of overall complex

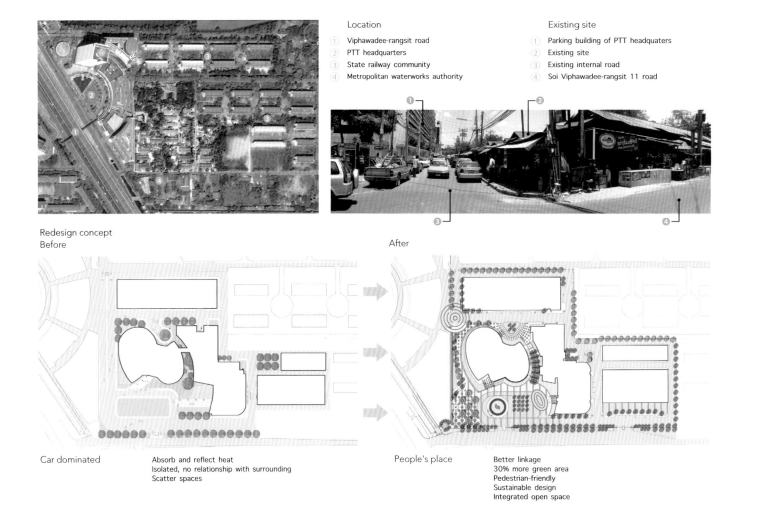

Location

1. Viphawadee-rangsit road
2. PTT headquarters
3. State railway community
4. Metropolitan waterworks authority

Existing site

1. Parking building of PTT headquaters
2. Existing site
3. Existing internal road
4. Soi Viphawadee-rangsit 11 road

Redesign concept
Before

After

Car dominated

Absorb and reflect heat
Isolated, no relationship with surrounding
Scatter spaces

People's place

Better linkage
30% more green area
Pedestrian-friendly
Sustainable design
Integrated open space

1. Common space between two buildings creates a comfortable area for variety of activities
2. Rest areas on 7th and 8th floors
3. Shade trees provided at the plaza between the two buildings creates a comfortable area for variety of activities

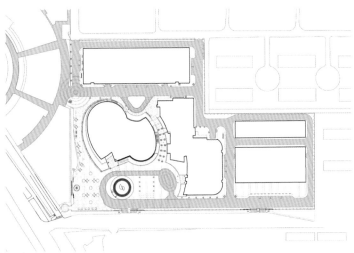

Vehicular

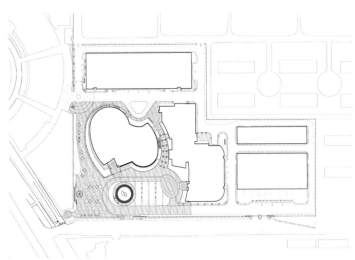

Pedestrian

Water-management system

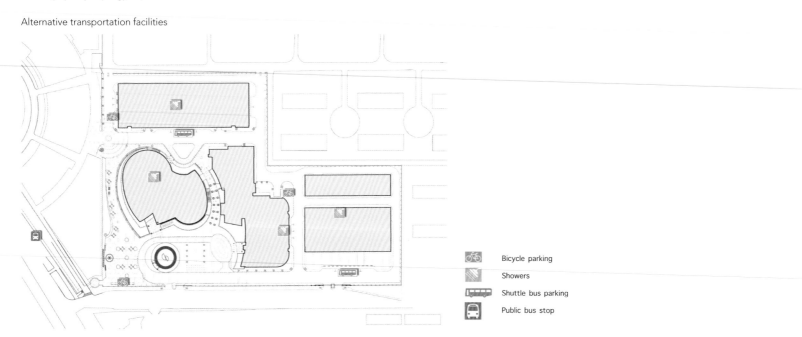

- Irrometers
- ( ) Stormwater barrels

Alternative transportation facilities

- Bicycle parking
- Showers
- Shuttle bus parking
- Public bus stop

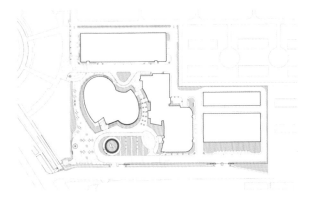

Green areas

Green roofs & roof gardens

① Green roof
② Roof garden

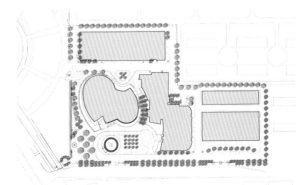

Trees plan

1. Irrigation system will automatically operate when moisture sensor detects a dry condition for each planting zone
2. Solar panel and planting area used on roof of the car park building
3. View to 7th and 8th floors from above

Note: Softscape concept

1. Total vegetated openspace is 287% more than required by BWA, and 50% more than required by LEED.
2. Roof gardens located on 8th and 9th floors of facilities building are used for recreation and outdoor exercise.
3. Green roofs on the rooftops of all parking buildings help to reduce heat absorption and harvest rainwater.
4. Native plants are good for easy adaptation and low water consumption.
5. Tree location helps to reduce heat, control wind direction and create 'comfort zone'.

1. Overall atmosphere of the complex at dusk
2. An interplay of building, sculpture and the sky
3. Brahma statue
4. Fountain and pool at the building base provide a smooth transition from the building to the grounds
5. Sunken court provides greenery and natural light for underground office space

1 | 4
2 | 3 | 5

Nature in Waldkirchen 2007

Nature in Waldkirchen, a new urban park, was developed on the southeastern edge of the old town. It is characterized by the natural landscape of the meadow valley.

The Waeschlbach valley features a variety of scenic and historic sites, such as the natural landmark Gsteinet, floodplain forests, and hillside meadows along Waeschlbach, as well as some protected habitats in an urban context. Along the elongated meadows, the manifold topographies and the diverse landforms were used to develop differentiated gardens and to provide great views into the landscape. Manifold views beyond the park borders enlarge the spatial impression of the park.

Within the structural facilities, the design respected the Waldkirchen´s location as part of the Bavarian Forest. Therefore, wood plays an important role as both a functional and artistic element. The elements of the urban park, such as the entrance square, urban promenade, water staircase, cherry gardens, pond, and Waeschlbach, as well as the spacious meadows with the Gsteinet, are designed as self-contained areas.

In the northern part of the entrance plaza, the piped Waeschlbach reaches the ground surface. The water runs down the approximately 13.1-foot-wide (4-meter-wide) staircase, which leads to the existing natural stream. The staircase is made of natural stone.

The Waeschlbach, which meanders through the valley, is embedded amid inclined meadows. The creek and the adjacent wet meadows provide space for an educational experience of nature and nature-loving activities. The visitor can have a look at the creek by walking on the little boardwalks that run along it. A natural clearing is the highlight.

A pond gives the visitor a natural and introverted impression on the east of the Waeschlbach. A wooden loop leads around the pond. Single common and planting areas in the form of seat capsules were designed along the path. Some of the seat capsules were technically equipped to make a restrained acoustic sound possible.

On the historic site of Waldkirchen's water reserve, the garden 'Bellevue' was newly interpreted by using instruments of contemporary landscape architecture. At 'Bellevue,' the unique view at Waldkirchen was used and staged through a self-contained design. On a spatial viewpoint, a water fountain was placed, which is a playground and recreational area. The water feature has single fountains, which can be operated and regulated by the visitor by pressing buttons on the 'Aquasonum.' Meanwhile, sounds can be generated the same way.

Location |
Waldkirchen, Germany
Site area |
18.5 acres (7.5 hectares)
Landscape design |
Rehwaldt LA
Client |
Natur in Waldkirchen 2007 GmbH
Photography |
Rehwaldt LA, Dresden

① Garden
② Underground car park
③ City gateway
④ Viewpoint
⑤ Kindergarten
⑥ Bench
⑦ Kindergarten playground
⑧ Play terraces
⑨ Schoolyard
⑩ School lawn
⑪ Viewing platform
⑫ Promenade
⑬ Planting
⑭ Meadow
⑮ Island
⑯ Reservoir
⑰ Jungle
⑱ Water ramp
⑲ Pond
⑳ Sidewalk
㉑ Floor lights
㉒ Wetlands

Master plan for the city park

1. View over city park and playground
2. Belvedere in the centre of city park
3. Trampoline
4. Climbing objects

4

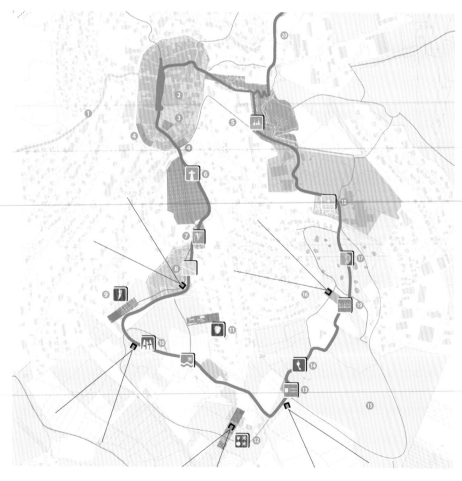

1. Golden sidewalk
2. Trade and exchange market place
3. Old cemetery
4. Walled garden
5. City park
6. Cemetery
7. Bellevue
8. The oblique garden
9. Sharp cake garden
10. Rock forest
11. Sweet cake garden
12. Garden of the four seasons
13. Karoli chapel
14. Barefoot forest
15. Karoli forest
16. Waldkirchen landscape
17. Ears forest
18. Muscle meadow
19. Art meadow
20. Connection to the station

The exposition 'nature in Waldkirchen' creates a new system of open spaces.

1. The main park axis
2. Relaxing area near the school
3. The park valley
4. Bridge over the Waeschl creek

1. Water stairs down in the park
2. Big park chair
3. Inside the climbing tree
4. Water basin with aquasonum sound generator
5. Aquasonum sound generator
6. Operate both music and water

Sainthorto with the H

Thanks to a special computer, Sainthorto can create in real time a musical composition by Vincenzo Core (and audio signals), starting from a single tune that will be worked out automatically according to homothetic principles. The music length is divided into multiples of two, leaving unchanged the length between musical notes. These new versions are located between four items that work on different logs.

The smaller the tune, the more it will be subjected to additional manipulations that will increase its complexity. Moreover, the length of musical notes determines the length of the different sections proportionally: short notes coincide with short moments characterized by small and dense melodic sounds, long notes coincide with rarefied and wide moments. When all the sections that coincide with the melody have been generated, it moves on to another melody: the 'microshape' instigates the next 'microshape. '

All sounds are generated in real time through subtractive synthesis and physical patterns synthesis. The music is then modulated on environmental variables captured by a weather station in the garden: the variations in wind speed create clusters of sounds, the temperature influences the timbre of the sounds, and the humidity changes the sound with echoes and reverberations.

The melody reveals itself through the human interaction. Sonic harps, provided with sensors that can detect the touch, are installed in the garden. The same sensors are also attached to some vegetables. If someone touches plant racks, harps, or vegetables, notes will be produced as improvised music. By touching once any plant racks, harps, or vegetables, in a few seconds the garden begins to resonate and plays a melody without any manipulation.

The Sainthorto project combines four strictly connected factors: functionality, aesthetics, production, and teaching. Production must be the cornerstone when one wants to design the layout, so that the useful surface for the cultivation changes according to its context.

Location |
Roma, Italy
Completion date |
2013
Site area |
1507 square feet (140 square meters)

Architecture and landscape design |
Francesco Lipari and Vanessa
Todaro (OFL Architecture)
+Federico Giacomarra
Client |
Maker Faire Rome
Photography |
Anotherstudio

1–2. View of Sainthorto at Maker Faire, 2013
3. Paraimpu station

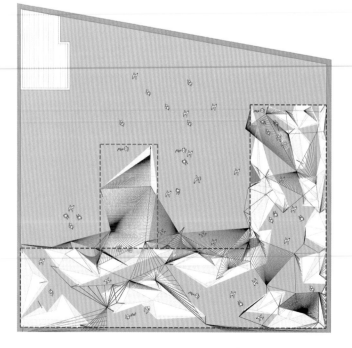

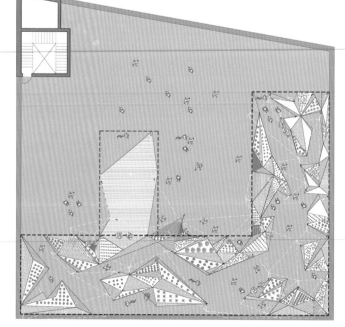

Plans

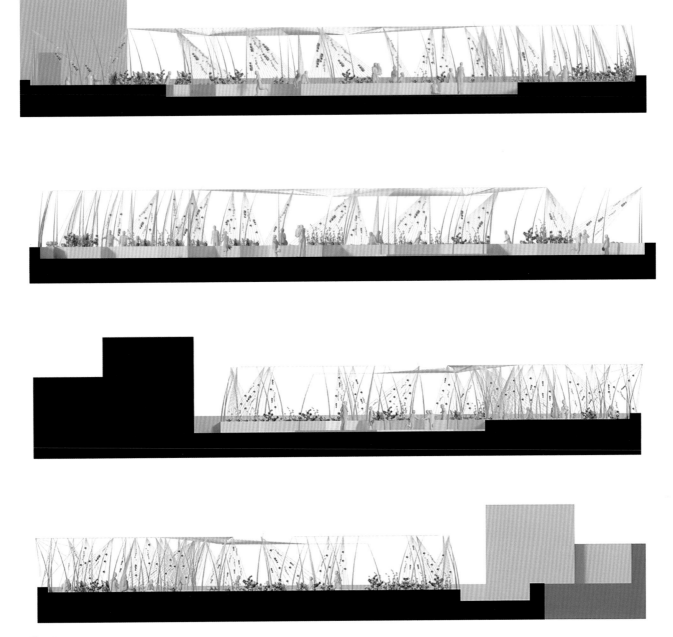

Elevations

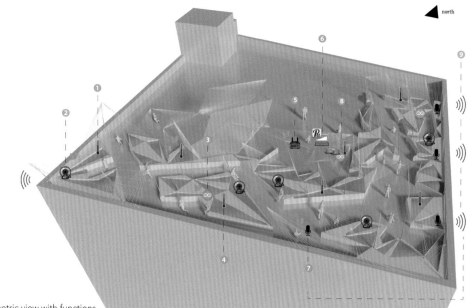

north

Axonometric view with functions

① Tanks sensor
   Ground humidity
② Ipcam (smartphone)
③ Arduino
   Data collector (max. 4 or 5 sensors)
④ Tanks sensor
   Ground humidity
⑤ Wi-Fi router
   To connect arduino and the ipcam/smatphone to internet
⑥ Mini-PC
   To aggregate data to send to paraimpu
⑦ Sound level meter
   To measure and sample sounds/vibrations made by the strings stimulated by the wind
⑧ Weather station
   To measure temperature, humidity and brightness
⑨ Lanificio concerts
   Sounds sampling / Vibrations by the strings for live concerts and ambient music

① Main entrance
② Educational path
③ Entrance/exit
④ Cultivation tank
⑤ Hemp white ropes
⑥ Cultivation tank
⑦ Temporary pavilion 16.4 by 16.4 foot (5 by 5 meters)
⑧ Educational area
⑨ Wood bench
⑩ Fir-tree pole
⑪ Hemp hammock

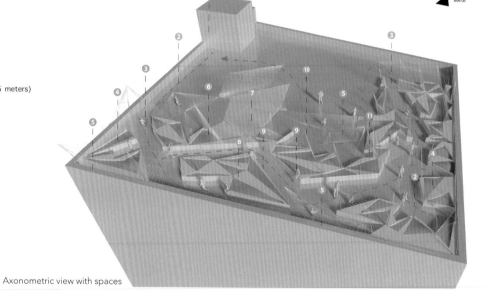

north

Axonometric view with spaces

1. Vases of Sainthorto
2. Proximity sensor
3. Detail of Sainthorto
4. A child playing with the interactive harps

2 | Intelligent Illumination and Intelligent Lighting

There are many energy-saving methods for landscaping illumination and intelligent lighting, and these could be generalized as below:

- Use highly efficient and energy-saving lighting sources.
- Use highly efficient and energy-saving lighting fixtures.
- Use a variety of control facilities for energy-saving lighting.
- Use sustainable electric power such as wind power and solar power.
- Use special architectural structure to lower demands for lighting.

For saving energy in landscaping, a monitoring system could be used to save energy resources. To reduce charges for electricity and maintenance fees of landscaping lighting, intelligent control measures can be taken to adjust and control the lighting system according to time periods. Through remote-monitoring, remote-controlling, and remote-adjusting of various lighting facilities, and flexible strategies for lighting control and time control, we can realize management and control in real time. Nowadays, street lights with wind power and solar power are often planned in the designing stage of landscaping. Energy can also be saved by optimal choice of natural light and reasonable use of solar power, wind power, and hydro power.

Autostadt Roof and Service Pavilion:
The roof structure produces greatest
possible lightness

TCS Garima Park:
Energy-saving light, and fountains in
night landscape

Wireless intelligent lighting system

Traditional lighting-control systems have many shortcomings, including troublesome wiring, rewiring in case of increases and decreases of equipment, weak expansibility of systems, and high costs for installation and maintenance. Therefore, wireless communication technology is an ideal choice for creating an intelligent lighting system. ZigBee technology offers a solution to make wireless intelligent lighting systems come true.

The ZigBee system has the ability to meet modern demands of landscaping lighting systems. The controller and lighting nodes of a wireless intelligent lighting system only require transmission on/off signals and lighting-adjusting signals. The system has low frequency of data transmission, while ZigBee's transmission rate can reach around 250 kilobytes per second, which is sufficient for the application of wireless intelligent lighting system. All lighting nodes in the system need to form a star, a cluster or a mesh network. The number of nodes may range from dozens to thousands. In a ZigBee network, the maximum number of nodes is 65,535, and it can support the structure outlined. Therefore, it can meet the requirements of wireless intelligent lighting systems for network structure and capacity. The system requires various nodes manufactured by different factories to be compatible; the ZigBee system meets international standards and can guarantee nodes developed by different factories are compatible and interchangeable, thus it can successfully reduce the cost of landscaping light tubes. In an intelligent lighting system, ZigBee can work at a ISM frequency range of 2.4 gigahertz, its signals have a certain penetrability (maximum communication distance between nodes can be 328.1 feet [100 meters]), and ZigBee

can support routing nodes. As long as the layout is reasonable, it can warrant that there is no dead zone of zero communication in a certain range. ZigBee is quick in response (a single data transmission process between two nodes can be finished in 5 milliseconds), which meets the real-time requirement of lighting systems. The lighting system is cost-sensitive and ZigBee is a low-bitrate, low-cost wireless-communication technology.

The network nodes of wireless intelligent lighting systems can be classified into coordinators, routers, and terminal nodes. The hardware structure of the coordinator is shown in diagram 4.

The vibration sensor and brightness sensor in the coordinator are used to detect vibration and brightness data in the site. When the vibration is weak, the vibration sensor recognizes that the work staff or visitors have left the site and automatically turns off the lights or turns down the brightness. When the lighting is too strong, such as on a sunny day, the brightness sensors can automatically reduce the brightness; when the lighting is too dark, such as at night or on a windy day, the brightness sensors will increase the brightness. The system only needs to integrate a vibration sensor and a brightness sensor in a node, then it can transmit controlling data to all lighting nodes through the ZigBee network. This way, it can intelligently control the whole lighting system and reduce electricity consumption.

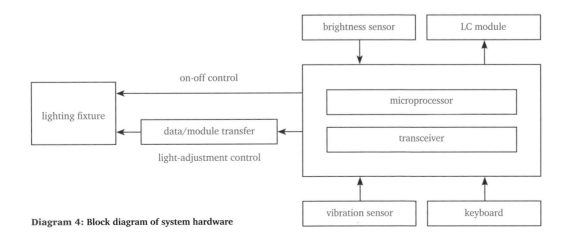

Diagram 4: Block diagram of system hardware

Intelligent lighting control system

In recent years, green energy has been widely used in landscaping designs. In them, intelligent lighting control systems have played an important role in green-energy systems. The solar-powered LED-lighting system as a major green energy has increasingly been applied in landscaping designs. Currently, this system has increasingly wide application in city plazas, theme parks, etc. The plaza landscaping lighting system based on wireless sensor networks introduced in this passage has achieved remote control over activation of LED lights, light intensity, and light color. It can flexibly construct several landscaping scenes; meanwhile it also inspects the work status of LED lights and their power supply in real time to ensure timely and efficient maintenance of the system.

The ZigBee wireless sensor network is a solar-energy lighting control system based on a sensor network; it is simple, reliable and easy to install. It can control the light intensity and color of intersystem lighting units. LED is characterized with low power consumption, long life, quick response, and easy lighting adjustment. Because of these, it has become an important choice in landscaping lighting design, particularly the solar-energy LED-lighting system; it has already found applications in landscaping areas such as streets, plazas, and parks.

The landscaping lighting system based on the ZigBee sensor network can monitor in real time, has centralized control, and manages the status of multiple lighting units in the system. The inspection and control communication mode of the system can guarantee coordinated switching of different scenes in real time. The system can reliably operate in landscaping such as city theme parks. It can be easily set for multiple scenes, and the scenes can be automatically and accurately switched over.

Landscaping lighting systems are mainly composed of three parts: lighting units, scene controllers, and a monitoring host computer as shown in diagram 5. With the monitoring host computer, staff of the landscaping lighting system can detect, manage, and control the operating state of the lighting units

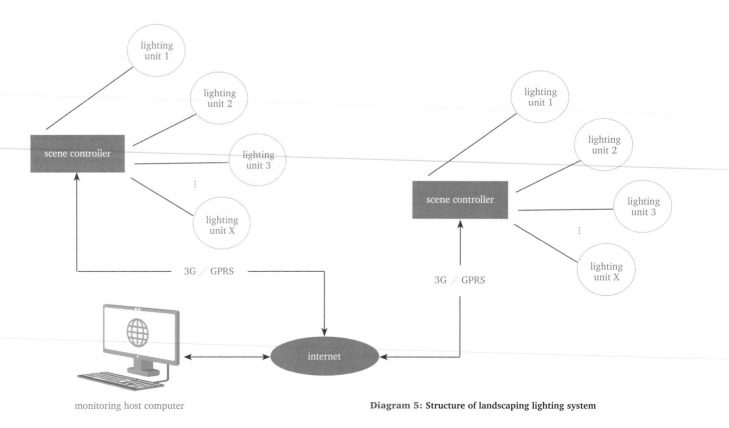

monitoring host computer

Diagram 5: Structure of landscaping lighting system

of the whole system. The host computer is connected to the internet and is installed with monitoring software. The scene controllers and the lighting units under their control are basic units of the system. The host computer communicates with the system through the internet and GPRS wireless network. The system makes decisions about the number of scene controllers according to the landscaping lighting scale and application environment. As landscaping lighting has lower requirements for real-time performance than an industrial control system, and has less demand for data transmission, the landscaping system partially uses ZigBee's wireless sensor network. The lighting units can perform the functions of sensor network equipment, while the scene controller can play the role of wireless sensor gateway, be the coordinator for each sensor network, and take responsibility for the networking of all sensors, and transmission and management of data. The lighting units of the system not only need to perform the functions of sensors, but also need to collect detection data of lighting units, send data in accordance with requirements of the system, and manage storage battery charging and lighting.

A lighting unit consists of five parts, namely solar panels (pack), power management modules, storage batteries (pack), LED-light control modules and wireless transceiver modules.

The scene controller has a built-in GPRS module, while the lighting unit can connect to the internet through the GPRS network to communicate with the upper computer. Meanwhile, the scene controller works as a coordinator in the ZigBee wireless sensor network, responsible for networking wireless sensors and managing all sensor facilities (lighting units).

When the system goes into operation, the scene controller's job is not to process and store data from the monitoring host and lighting units, but to directly transmit the inspected data from lighting units to the monitoring host through LAN. When receiving data, the monitoring host will process them and send instructions to each lighting unit through the scene controller. As a gateway for sensors in the system, the scene controller is responsible for communicating with the equipment and internet.

The monitoring host functions as the data center of the whole landscaping lighting system, taking responsibility for processing and accessing data from multiple scenes and lighting units in the system. When the system is operating, the software of the upper computer will receive status data of lighting units, transmitted from scene controllers through the internet, and then

it will send orders of inquiry and setting to the scene controller according to demand, while the scene controller will forward the data to the corresponding lighting units.

The monitoring host is the control center of the system, controlling the starting time, light color, and light intensity of all lighting units in the system. The system is set up on the basis of scene controllers, which can allocate parameters for each lighting unit. The software offers editing functions and can code the edited texts and store them in a local hard-disk file. The setting plus the starting and ending times will be sent to the specified scene controller. At the same time, the software of the monitoring upper computer can analyze the operating status of the system, and recognize when maintenance is required.

The ZigBee wireless sensor network is a low-bitrate, low-power-consumption and short-distance wireless communication technology, and can support multiple networking forms; therefore, it is adopted by landscaping lighting control systems. Considering efficiency and reliability, landscaping lighting control systems use star topological networks; that means each landscaping lighting system shall be deployed by at least one scene controller according to requirements. Each scene controller directly communicates with lighting units. As each sensor network has only one scene controller and each scene controller is responsible for a single sensor network, the system's monitoring host needs to manage several scene controllers through the internet.

Indochina Villas Saigon

The Indochina Villas Saigon experience begins with the statement at its entrance on the main road. Inspired by rice patterns, the boundary wall is unique in creating a strong identity and character. The boundary wall merges with the art wall—the most important feature of the entry. The wall, with sculpted patterns with deep shadows, changes character in the evening when the light box behind the wall softly glows to create a dramatic effect.

The rice-inspired pattern unifies and manifests itself on a series of scales throughout the project, especially in the community pool area located just past the entrance. Designed as the key gathering place, this area visually connects the adjacent lake with its infinity swimming pool featuring a linear deck canopy structure. With its patterned panels providing horizontal and vertical support, it is an elegant structure with sculptural qualities. A shaded corridor of similar design character connects the Tai Chi Plaza with the waterfront barbecue deck and children's water fountain. Inspired by the lotus and conceived as a feature play fountain, the sculptural installation is more an artwork than a water feature. Dramatic lighting in this area highlights the sculptural elements and brings a boutique resort feel to the development.

Further down the development is the neighborhood park, the other key park space within the project. Conceived as a green oasis, and accessed from the linear waterfront park, it is a space with many unique features. The shape and pattern inspired by the geometrical abstraction of the rice grain find new forms, the most common being the feature screen. Set against lush planting, the screens create a new setting within this park. A series of platforms with benches provides places for relaxation and contemplation. The park also contains a central floating canopy hovering among the tree layer, its elegant floating plane in complete contrast to the tree foliage. Supported by a series of slender metal columns, the canopy's sculptural quality is further enhanced by a series of cut-outs in shapes of the pattern, not only to reduce the weight but also to create an exciting play of shadows on the ground. A series of stepping stones on the lawn in the same geometric shape adds unity to the theme, and turns the illusion of the pavilion cut-out shadows into actual stepping stones on the ground. A series of sculptural seats as extrusions of the geometric shape appear among the greenery, contrasting against the backdrop of lush foliage. LED lighting further creates drama in highlighting these key landscape features within the park.

The landscape designer's approach of integrating art and culture in this project creates a unique landscape to be enjoyed by residents and visitors, making Indochina Villas Saigon a landmark development in Ho Chi Minh City and creating a new benchmark in resort-style city living.

Location |
Ho Chi Minh City, Vietnam
Completion date |
2014
Site area |
19.8 acres (8 hectares)
Landscape design |
One Landscape Design Ltd
Client |
Indochina Land
Photography |
Jason Findley, Aaron Joel Santos

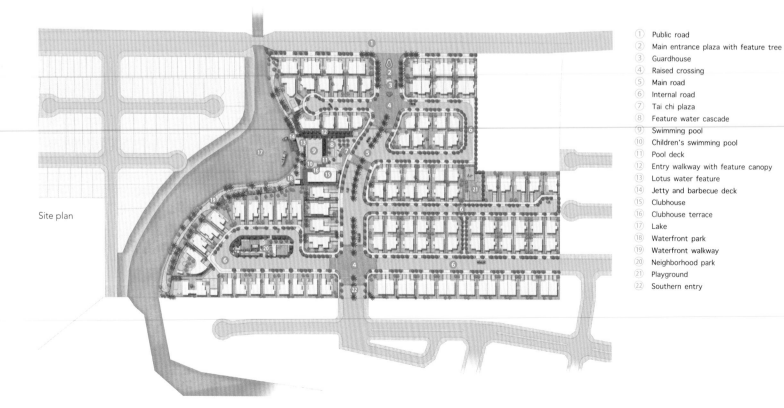

Site plan

① Public road
② Main entrance plaza with feature tree
③ Guardhouse
④ Raised crossing
⑤ Main road
⑥ Internal road
⑦ Tai chi plaza
⑧ Feature water cascade
⑨ Swimming pool
⑩ Children's swimming pool
⑪ Pool deck
⑫ Entry walkway with feature canopy
⑬ Lotus water feature
⑭ Jetty and barbecue deck
⑮ Clubhouse
⑯ Clubhouse terrace
⑰ Lake
⑱ Waterfront park
⑲ Waterfront walkway
⑳ Neighborhood park
㉑ Playground
㉒ Southern entry

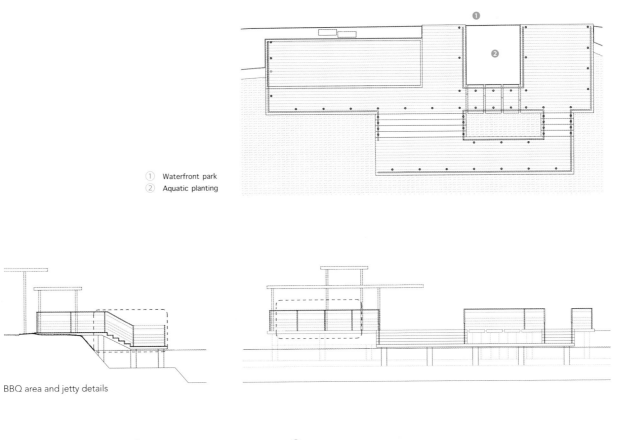

① Waterfront park
② Aquatic planting

BBQ area and jetty details

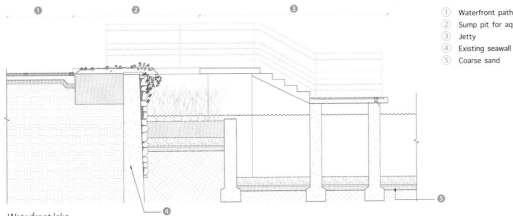

① Waterfront path
② Sump pit for aquatic planting
③ Jetty
④ Existing seawall
⑤ Coarse sand

Waterfront lake

1. The floating BBQ pavilion and jetty hover above the pristine lake
2. The view of the spectacular promenade along the lake

1. The aerial view of the club pool with feature canopy
2. The rice shape–inspired feature screen as artwork in the park
3. Set against lush planting, the feature screen as geometric abstraction of rice pattern

1 | 2 / 3

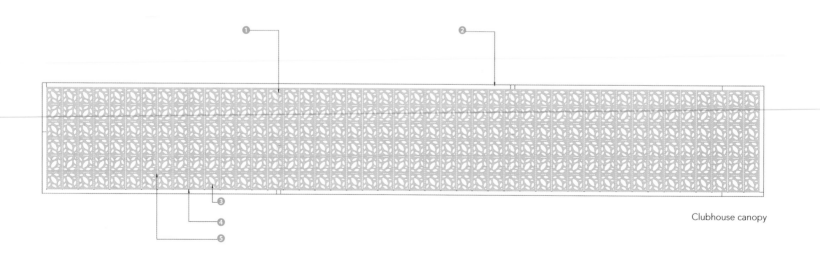

Clubhouse canopy

① 3.94 x 3.94 inch (100 x 100 millimeter) RHS beam finish to match with screen panels as per engineer's specifications and details
② 5.91 x 3.94 inch (150 x 100 millimeter) RHS roof frame finish to match with screen panels as per engineer's specifications and details
③ Laser-cut aluminum panel as per specialist's details and specifications timber finish
④ Steel-L 0.79 x 0.0.39 inch (20 x 10 millimeter) frame as per specialist's details and specifications
⑤ Steel-T 0.79 x 0.0.39 inch (20 x 10 millimeter) frame as per specialist's details and specifications

Feature screen

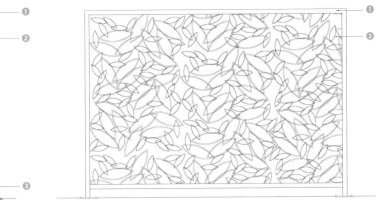

① 1.97 x 1.97 inch (50 x 50 millimeter) RHS frame
② 0.39-inch (10-millimeter) cast-iron grain pattern to be welded on RHS frame bronze powder coated finish
③ 0.39-inch (10-millimeter) metal plate welded
④ R.C. footing by engineer's specification

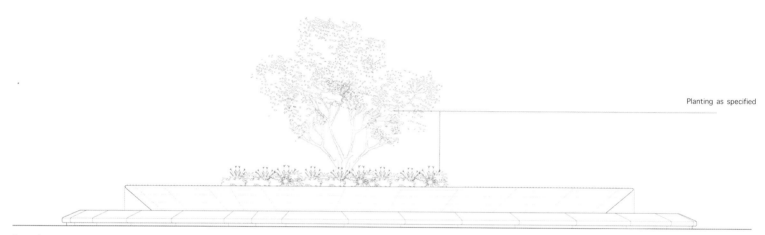

Planting as specified

Tree plan

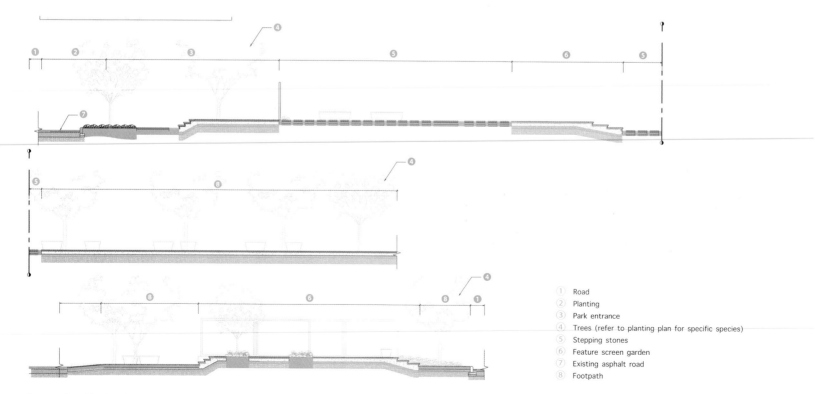

① Road
② Planting
③ Park entrance
④ Trees (refer to planting plan for specific species)
⑤ Stepping stones
⑥ Feature screen garden
⑦ Existing asphalt road
⑧ Footpath

Section of neighborhood park

1. A shaded seating area under the feature canopy for viewing and contemplation
2. The layering of hardscape and softscape elements within the park
3. The rice shape of the canopy create poetic play of shadows on the ground
4. The lotus sculpture as children's water-play installation

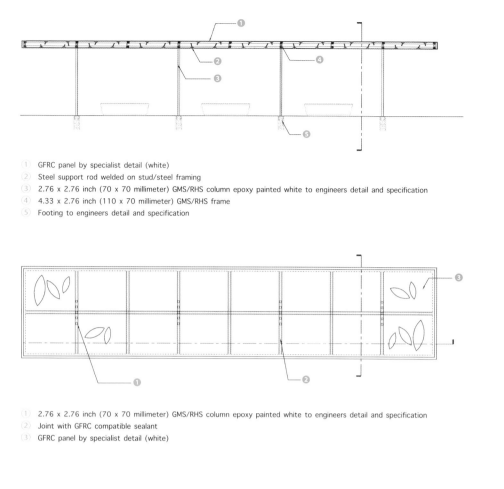

(1) GFRC panel by specialist detail (white)

(2) Steel support rod welded on stud/steel framing

(3) 2.76 x 2.76 inch (70 x 70 millimeter) GMS/RHS column epoxy painted white to engineers detail and specification

(4) 4.33 x 2.76 inch (110 x 70 millimeter) GMS/RHS frame

(5) Footing to engineers detail and specification

(1) 2.76 x 2.76 inch (70 x 70 millimeter) GMS/RHS column epoxy painted white to engineers detail and specification

(2) Joint with GFRC compatible sealant

(3) GFRC panel by specialist detail (white)

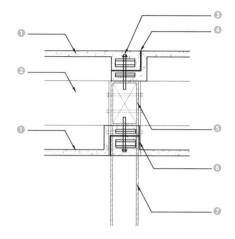

(1) GFRC panel by specialist detail (white)

(2) GMS/RHS frame

(3) GRFC anchor by manufacturer

(4) Joint with GFRC compatible sealant

(5) 4.33 x 2.76 inch (110 x 70 millimeter) GMS/RHS frame

(6) Steel plate welded and bolted

(7) 2.76 x 2.76 inch (70 x 70 millimeter) GMS/RHS column epoxy painted white to engineers detail and specification

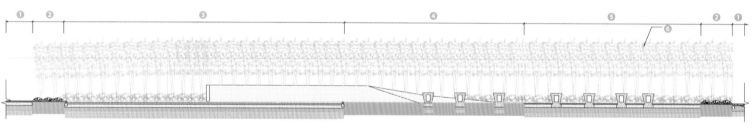

(1) Sidewalk

(2) Planting

(3) Safety mat area

(4) Lawn area

(5) Seating area

(6) Bamboo planting (refer to planting plan for specific species)

Playground section

1. The rice shape–inspired feature screen as artwork in the park
2. The elegant floating canopy hovers among the trees and the greenary
3. The project experience begins with the entry statement and its frontage to the main road
4. The interplay of light as part of the art wall

① 5.91 x 1.97 inches (150 x 50 millimeters) RHS bronze powder coated
② Concrete wall with 0.79-inch (20-millimeter) white render
③ 1.97-inch (50 millimeter) light grey stone
④ Built-up letters in bronze powder coated finish

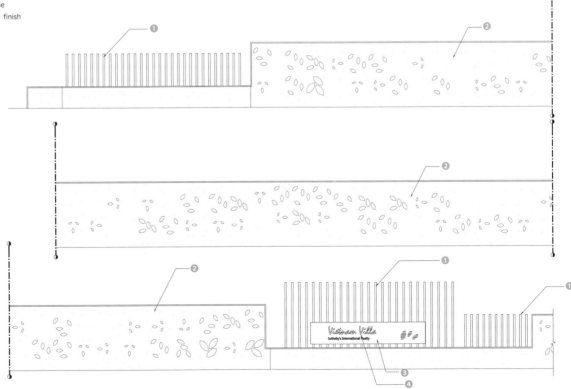

Main entrance feature wall details

Water cascade

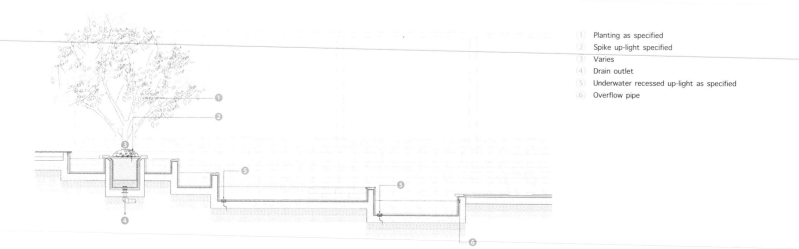

(1) Planting as specified
(2) Spike up-light specified
(3) Varies
(4) Drain outlet
(5) Underwater recessed up-light as specified
(6) Overflow pipe

1. The rich landscape seting of the villa
2. The juxtapostion of organic with inorganic, artificial with natural
3. The play area and the garden
4. The rich patterned panels as both horizontal and vertical elements of the elegant pool canopy
5. The interplay of steps and water cascade

Autostadt Roof and Service Pavilion

Driver assistance systems, including automatic parking, traffic-sign recognition and automatic distance control, are becoming more common in today's cars. The new 'Ausfahrt' at the Autostadt in Wolfsburg offers guests an opportunity to try out these technical systems in models manufactured by Volkswagen. This helps to ensure safer driving on the road. Covering 161,459 square feet (15,000 square meters), the new driving attraction was built in 10 months and opened in August 2013.

Graft Gesellschaft von ArchitektenmbH I (GRAFT) was commissioned to create a quiet area where the buyer of a new car could get familiar with all the functions in an almost private atmosphere. The space had to be protected from rain and direct sunlight, while allowing enough daylight to avoid the use of expensive and unnecessary artificial light.

GRAFT developed the idea of a horizontal leaf that protects the landscape underneath with its organic form. WES LandschaftsArchitektur planned the landscape surrounding the roof. As the roof follows the concept of a leaf, the pavilion is integrated into the architectural landscape and not designed as a separate building. Basic forms of the roof can be found in the interior architecture.

In the architectural application of this structure, it was necessary to produce the greatest possible lightness: a special static principle allows for the unique roof structure to be anchored in just two points. It lays in the landscape and defines a clear and protected room. The planning of the structural framework was done by Schlaich Bergmann und Partner.

The orientation of the roof represents a welcoming gesture through its curvature. The elegant amorphous geometry of the roof structure forms a bridge between top and bottom, between sky and landscape.

The associated service pavilion fulfills various functions: the customer can ask questions about the new car, purchase accessories, or get information about Volkswagen Autostadt attractions and activities.

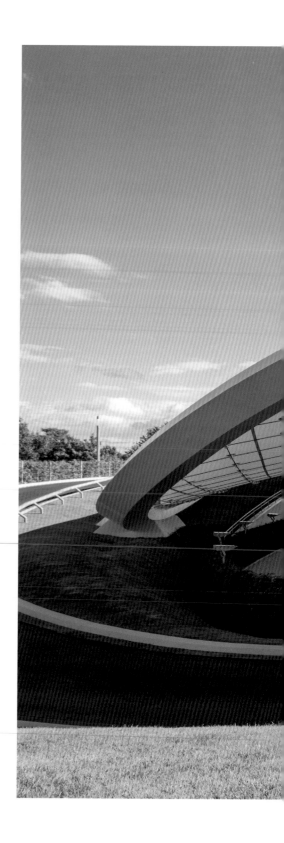

Location |
Wolfsburg, Germany
Completion date |
2013
Architect |
Graft Gesellschaft von Architekten mbH
Planning of the structural framework |
Schlaich Bergermann und Partner
Landscape design |
WES LandschaftsArchitektur I

Contractor for roof structure |
Eiffel Deutschland
Stahltechnologie GmbH
Client |
Autostadt Wolfsburg
Photography |
WES LandschaftsArchitektur,
Tobias Hein

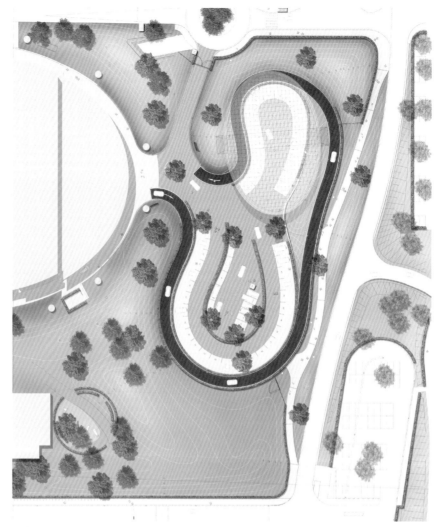

Bird's-eye view

1. Arriving at Autostadt Roof and Service Pavilion
2. Weather-protection roof structure in Wolfsburg, Germany
3. The horizontal leaf protects the landscape underneath with its organic form

1. Structural *Details inside the Roof*
2. A special static principle allows for the unique roof structure to be anchored in just two points
3. The *Roof Structure* lies in the landscape and defines a clear and protected room
4. Inside the *Service Center*
5. The service center flooded with light

1	4
2	3	5

TCS Garima Park

The design of the software center is based on the single workstation unit and its need for optimal light. Everything revolves around the workstations housed in the central block. Ten thousand are accommodated; the design allows for 20 percent more workstations without the need for an additional building. These would be accommodated on mezzanine floors in the east block.

Climatic principles of location, orientation, and other site issues were considered. The direction of entry, placement of the main block in the center, and the location of other functions correspond to the design of a previous building for this company. The building follows *vastu* principles and is perfectly attuned to Ahmedabad's climate.

In the landscape elements of TCS Garima Park, interlocking paver blocks have been used extensively in pathways throughout the campus. Other materials include shot-blasted limestone, which have been used in the hardscaped walkways and plazas. Several pergolas have also been incorporated into the design, which have been made in either solid wood or ferro-cement with an imitate wood finish, providing shade and a resting space for people, as well as creating an interplay of shadow and light. Several bodies of water such as fountains have been included in the design proposal, enhancing the overall feel of the park. An amphitheater is proposed for the northeast side, providing a space for interaction and gathering for the employees.

TCS Garima Park has been developed as a 'green' campus and has applied for a LEED (Leadership in Energy and Environmental Design) Gold rating. Solar panels, LED lighting, and occupancy and light-sensitive sensors have been used to optimize power consumption.

Location |
Gandhinagar, India
Completion date |
2009
Landscape design |
Snehal Shah with Engineering Design and
Research Center (Larsen & Toubro)
Landscape consultant |
Kishore D Pradhan

Client |
Tata Consultancy Services Ltd
Photography |
Snehal Shah with Engineering
Design and Research Centre,
Enrico Cano, Antonio Martinelli

1. Front east façade and front view of the park as seen from pond
2. Relaxed people on promenade way in the garden
3. Fountain panorama
4. Grass amphitheatre
5. Road between the park and forest

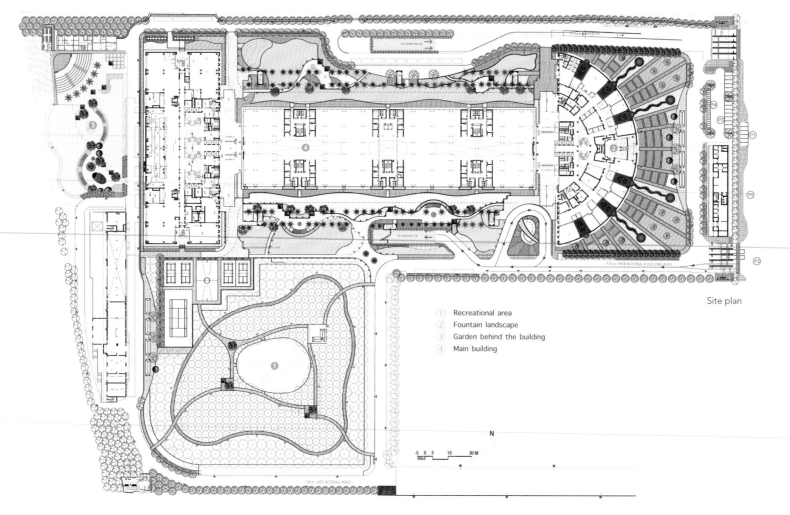

Site plan

1. Recreational area
2. Fountain landscape
3. Garden behind the building
4. Main building

N

-5 0 5   15   30 M

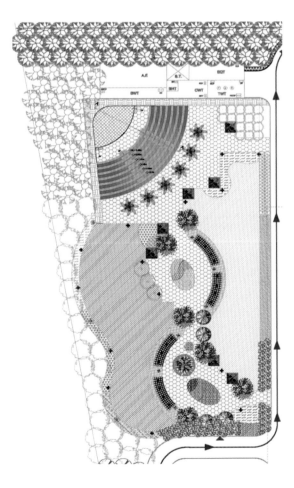

Area outside block 1

Area outside block 2

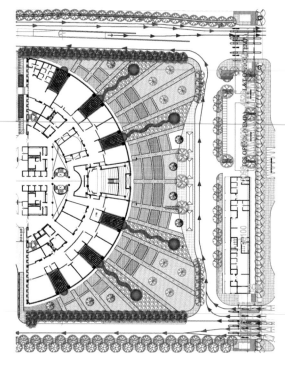

Water-fountain details

Post top lights

Gemini global bollards   Street light   Walkover

1. Fountains and front east façade at the entrance to the campus
2. Night scene of fountain and lighting of landscape
3. Side view of the park and north façade

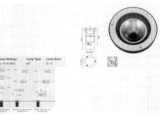

Down Lighter

Parking lights   Plant uplighter

Green enrichment mass planting

Alstonia scholaris

Anthocephalus kadamba

Brassia actinophylla

Bauhinia blackie

Cassia fistula

Cassia renegera

Plumeria rubra ornamental
character

Plumeria singapore ornamental
character

Tabebuia rosea

Green enrichment mass planting

Thevetia nerifolia

Hymenocallis littoralis

Zephyranthus lily

Green enrichment-mass planting
cordia sebestena

Michelia fragrancechampaca

Mussaenda frondosa native
forest species

Crinum lily variegates

St. augustine grass

Millingtonia horetnsis fragrance

Plumeria alba

Spathodea companulata colourful
flowers

Green enrichment palms

Acasia auriculiformis

Melia azederachta

Gliricidia maculata

Arecastrum romanzzofianum

Butia capitata

Phoenix kharek

Raphis palm

Raphis palm variegated

Acalypha tahiti colourful foliage

Acasia mangium

Alpinia purpurata

Tabernaemontana variegata

Tecoma gaudichaudi

Verbena mauve

Acalypha red colourful foliage

Bauhinia acuminata

Calliandra emarginata

Tecomaria capensis pink

Tecomaria capensis orange

Tecomaria capensis yellow

Excoecaria bicolor

Heliconia lanceana

Meyenia erecta miniature

Ixora duffii

Ixora miniature red colourful flowers

Kopsia fruticosa

Nerium oleander petit salmon

Pseudocalymma alliaceum colourful flowers

Quisqualis indica

Lagerstromia indica

Lantata gold mound

Lantana hybrid red

Allamanda neriifolia

Alpinia variegata colourful foliage

Bilbergia

Ruellia pink

Ruellia purple

Ruellia white

Duranta sunshine

Duranta golden

Eranthemum laxiflorum

Tabernaemontana coronaria

Tabernaemontana double dwarf

Tabernaemontana single dwarf

Excoecaria bicolor

Heliconia lanceana

Heliconia psittacorum

Graptophyllum pictum

Hamelia patens

Hibiscus minimarvel

3 | Wind-power Technology

It is estimated that there are about 10 billion kilowatts of wind power generated around the world per year, which is nearly 10 times the amount of hydropower currently generated around the globe. Presently, the power acquired globally each year by burning coal is only one-third of the amount of wind power produced. Therefore, wind power as a new energy resource has attracted the attention of nations. Meanwhile, as wind-power-generating facilities have a unique appearance, they are sometimes treated as a landscaping element. They can provide electric power for normal operation of landscaping and reduce the demands for non-renewable energy resources in landscaping.

Structure of a wind-power generator

Wind-power generation refers to the processes that transform wind kinetic power into mechanical kinetic power, and then turn the latter into electric kinetic power. Its work principle is to rotate the windmill blades by wind, then use a machine to increase the rotating speed and promote the generator to generate power. A wind-power generator, also named a windmill, is a machine that turns wind power into mechanical power. The structure of a wind-power generator is quite complicated, mainly composed of the following parts:

Nacelle

The nacelle mainly accommodates major equipment of the wind-power generator, including a gearbox and a generator. Maintenance staff can enter the nacelle through the generator's tower.

Rotor blades

The rotor blades can catch wind and transfer wind force to the axis of the rotor. For a 600 kilowatt wind-power generator, each rotor blade is around 65 feet (20 meters) long, often designed to resemble the propeller of airplanes.

Rotor axis

The rotor axis is a device attached to the low-speed shaft of the wind-power generator.

Low-speed shaft

The rotor axis and gearbox of the wind-power generator are connected with each other by a low-speed shaft. For a 600 kilowatt wind-power generator, the rotor's speed is as low as about 19–30 turns per minute. The low-speed shaft has an internal conduit for the hydraulic system, which could be used to activate an aerodynamic brake.

High-speed shaft and mechanical brake

The high-speed shaft operates at a speed of 1500 turns per minute and drives the generator. An emergency mechanical brake is installed in the high-speed shaft and goes into operation when the aerodynamic brake fails or when the generator is being maintained.

Gearbox

The gearbox can increase the rotating speed of the high-speed shaft to as much as 50 times that of the low-speed shaft.

Generator

The generator is usually called an induction generator or an asynchronous generator. Nowadays, the most widely used generators often have a maximum electric output of 500–1500 kilowatts.

Yawning device

The yawning device relies on an electromotor to rotate the nacelle and thus make the rotor directly face the wind. The yawning device is operated by an electronic controller, which can detect wind direction by a wind indicator. Usually, when the wind changes direction, the wind-power generator deflects only a few degrees at a time.

Electronic controller

The electronic controller includes a computer that constantly monitors the state of the wind-power generator and controls the yawning device. To prevent mechanical failures (such as overheating of the gearbox or generator), the controller can automatically shut down the wind-power generator; it will then alert operation staff of the generator through a modem.

Hydraulic system

The hydraulic system is mainly used for resetting the aerodynamic brake of the wind-power generator.

Cooling unit

The cooling unit includes a mechanical fan and an oil-cooling unit. The former is mainly used for cooling the generator while the latter cools oil in the gearbox.

Tower

The tower contains the nacelle and the rotor. Generally speaking, a tall tower has an advantage because the wind grows stronger with increases of height. At present, the tower height for a 600 kilowatt wind turbine is 130–200 feet (40–60 meters). It could be a tube-like tower or a grid tower. A tube-like tower is safer for working staff as they can climb the internal ladder to the tower top. The grid tower has the advantage of relatively low cost.

Anemometer and wind indicator

The anemometer and wind indicator are devices for measuring wind speed and wind direction.

Types of wind-power generator

Cage asynchronous generator

The cage asynchronous generator is the most traditional generator in wind-power generation. Its motor rotor, on the whole, has a relatively high level of strength and rigidity. It is well suited for wind generation, but is not efficient and not able to effectively use wind power (see diagram 6).

Wound-rotor asynchronous generator

A wound-rotor asynchronous generator is constructed by connecting a motor rotor with a variable resistor. It can operate at limited variable speed and improve output power, meanwhile it can adjust pitch angle and control rotor current to enhance dynamic performance, maintain the stability of output power, and reduce the disturbance of gust to power grid (see diagram 7).

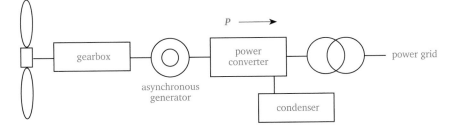

Diagram 6: Structural diagram of a cage asynchronous generator system

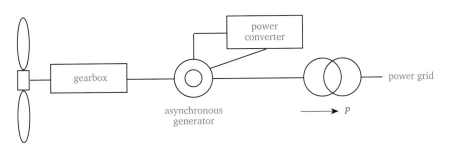

Diagram 7: Structural diagram of a wound-rotor asynchronous generator

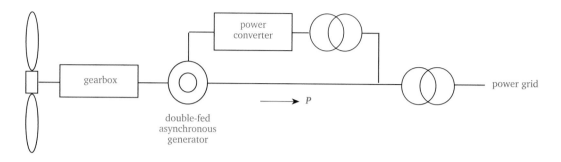

Diagram 8: Structural diagram of a double-fed asynchronous generator

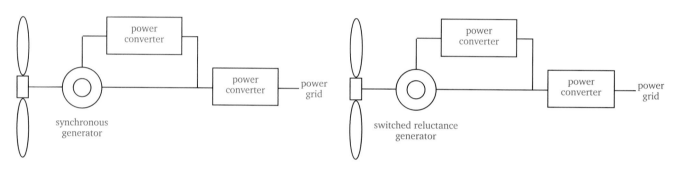

Diagram 9: Structural diagram of synchronous generator   **Diagram 10: Structural diagram of switched reluctance generator**

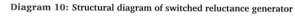

Brush double-fed asynchronous generator

Double-fed asynchronous generators can realize double-fed speed regulation by controlling slip frequency and are widely used in wind-power generating systems. However, this type of generator has a brush structure and is less reliable, thus it needs regular maintenance and is not suitable for application in harsh environments (see diagram 8).

Brushless double-fed asynchronous generator

The basic principle of the brushless double-fed asynchronous generator is the same as that of a brush double-fed asynchronous generator. The major difference is that it has canceled the electric brush and thus makes up for shortcomings of standard double-fed generators. Brushless double-fed asynchronous generators draw upon the merits of both cage asynchronous generators and wound-rotor asynchronous generators. Their power coefficients and operation speed are adjustable, and are fit for wind-power generator systems at variable speeds and constant frequency.

Synchronous generator

The synchronous generator has a varied numbers of poles, low rotation speed, big radial dimension, and small axial dimensions. When connected with an electronic power converter, it can achieve variable speed; therefore, it is applicable to wind-power generation systems. This type of generator also has the virtues of little noise, low flickering of power grid voltage, and a high power coefficient (see diagram 9).

Switched reluctance generator

The switched reluctance generator is characterized with a simple structure, high-energy tension, strong overload capacity, good static and dynamic performance, high reliability, and efficiency. When it is applied in wind-power generation systems, it has a big starting torque and excellent low-speed performance, and is often adopted in small wind-power generation systems with power less than 30 kilowatts (see diagram 10).

Permanent-magnet brushless DC generator

The permanent-magnet brushless DC generator uses a diode in place of an electric brush. It not only has the stable voltage waveform of DC generators, but also has advantages of high efficiency and long life of permanent-magnet synchronous generators. It is applicable to small wind-power generation systems.

Permanent-magnet synchronous generator

A permanent-magnet synchronous generator dispenses with reversing devices; therefore it has high efficiency and long life. This type of generator is only one-third the size of general generators, and one-fifth the weight. As this generator has more poles and integrated advantages of both synchronous motors and permanent-magnetic motors, it is suitable for connected grid forms with the generator directly connected to wind turbines and without a transmission mechanism.

All permanent-suspension wind-driven generator

An all permanent-suspension wind-power generator is completely composed of permanent magnets and without any control system. Meanwhile, the optimization design includes parts such as magnetic bearings, rotating shafts, fan stator coils, permanent magnetic rotors, and wind vanes, thus the generator is an integrated innovation. Compared with traditional wind-power generators, all permanent-suspension wind-power generators can really 'start with a breeze and generate power with gentle wind'. They can develop low-speed resources around the globe and increase annual power generation.

Intelligent control of wind-power generator

Fuzzy control

Fuzzy control is a typical approach of intelligent control. Its most remarkable feature is to express experts' experience and knowledge in rules that could be used for control. It doesn't rely on the subject's exact mathematical model, so it can overcome the influences of non-linear factors and maintain its integrity when applied to other subjects. As the wind-power generation system is a random non-linear system, fuzzy control is appropriate for the control of wind turbines. Fuzzy control has relatively good control over aspects such as tracking of the generator's speed, catchment of maximum wind energy, acquisition of maximum power rate, and robustness of the wind-power generating system.

A simplified fuzzy logic controller includes four parts: an input interface, a decision rule matrix, an inference engine, and an output interface.

The strategy of fuzzy logic control could be realized through the following steps:

- input control variables (text control variables)
- fuzzify text control variables through proper fuzzy membership functions
- determine control strategy by rule-based judgment matrix (heuristic rules)
- defuzzify output control variables through setting fuzzy assembling forms
- feed back output signals and control the operation of the wind-power generator through appropriate regulators.

Neural networks control

An artificial neural network has the non-linear mapping capability that can arbitrarily approach any non-linear models. As it has the capability of self-learning and self-convergence, it can be used as a good self-adaptive controller. In the wind-power generation system, the neural network can be applied in aspects such as predicting changes of wind direction on the basis of past wind-speed data. Data-based machine learning is an important aspect of modern intelligent technology. Researchers begin with finding rules from observed data and then use these rules to predict future data or non-observable data, and thus realize effective control over industrial processes.

Corpus Christi Bayfront

Following a devastating Category 4 hurricane in 1919 that destroyed its downtown, Corpus Christi filled in part of the Corpus Christi Bay to construct a new seawall that would protect the community from future disasters. Since that time, the bayfront has been defined by Shoreline Drive—a wide boulevard designed primarily for automobiles—and allocated limited spaces for pedestrians in the hot southern Texas sun.

North Bayfront Park is designed to accommodate festivals and events such as Buccaneer Days. Shoreline Boulevard is closed to traffic for these events to make space for performances, vendors, and pedestrians. Speed bumps, extended curbs, and reduced lanes curtail traffic and improve the street for pedestrians. The project promotes reuse of urban land and provides open space for all. Its sustainability features include the use of alternative power, innovative rainwater and stormwater management, reduced water requirements, and the use of native plants.

The park includes 35-foot-tall (10.7-meter-tall) wind turbines along the waterfront that are designed to produce energy that goes back into the grid. The wind turbines are also a form of kinetic art, with sculptural qualities derived from the shape and color of conch shells that express the city's distinctive setting on the bay. The turbines will serve as iconic landmarks on the waterfront as well as provide renewable energy to the park. The introduction of wind-power production also makes a cultural and historical connection by harnessing potentially harmful winds.

The park is sited atop the fill material behind the seawall constructed after the hurricane. Rainwater from the site is directed to a linear rain garden planted with native coastal meadow plants that filter stormwater contaminants, and allow water to seep into the ground. The coastal meadow serves as a reminder to visitors of the coastal landscape prior to the construction of the seawall, and provides information on the bay's ecology.

A key feature of the park is an interactive fountain, designed to appeal to children and families. Parents can sit at the adjacent café in the park, protected from the wind by glass screens, while watching their children play in the fountain. The café is shaded by fabric stretched between posts, while groves of palms and mesquite trees will grow over time to provide shady spots in the park. An arbor is designed to support colorful bougainvillea plantings that shade a walkway leading to the fountain. The arbor fronts a parcel of land intended for a future restaurant, included in the design.

Location |
Corpus Christi, Texas, United States
Completion date |
2010
Site area |
2.5 acres (1 hectare)
Landscape design |
Sasaki
Photography |
Eddie Seal, Haas-Anderson Construction

Sustainable features:
• promotes reuse of urban land
• provides open space for all
• employs alternative power
• uses innovative rain/stormwater management
• promotes health of the watershed
• requires reduced amounts of water for landscape
• employs native plant materials.

$\frac{1}{\frac{2}{3}} \Big| \frac{4}{5}$

1. Corpus Christi's Bayfront Park includes 35-foot wind turbines along the waterfront designed to supply the park's energy needs. Inspired by conch shells, they serve as iconic landmarks and kinetic art
2. The coastal meadow serves as a reminder of the seaside landscape and offers environmental education of the native landscape ecology of the bay
3. North Bayfront Park is designed to accommodate festivals, performances, fairs, and events
4. A key feature of the park includes an interactive fountain to attract children and families
5. The relocation, reduction of two travel lanes, and removal of the 80-foot-wide median of Shoreline Boulevard recaptured the bayfront land and allowed for the creation of North Bayfront Park

1 | 2

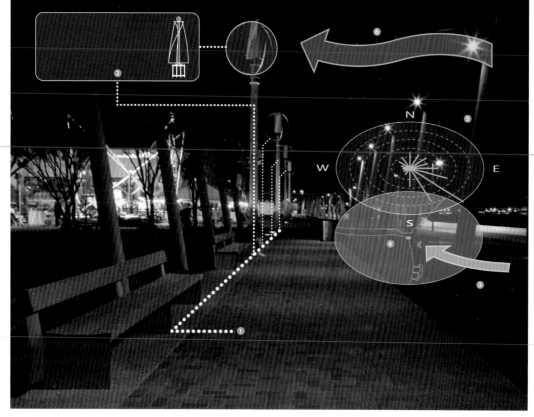

1　Four turbines create 4,730 kilowatts per year, a value of approximately $473
2　Gale-5 vertical axis turbine generates 130 watts in 12 mph winds and 1138.8 kilowatts each year
3　Dominant winds
4　Park site
5　Annual wind rose
6　Average annual wind-speed: 12 mph

Functional plan 1

1. A continuous walkway along the shoreline allows for increased public access to the waterfront and highlights existing architecture along Shoreline Drive
2. North Bayfront Park is the first of a series of parks to be constructed from the Sasaki master plan

Native coastal grasses rain garden collects stormwater runoff from 2 acres (0.8 hectares) of park and filters 90 percent of contaminates from the first inch of rain

Site runoff

Precipitation

Functional plan 2

Jan Feb Mar Apr May Jun Jul Aug Sept Oct Nov Dec

Low-Maintenance Eco-Campus of Vanke Architecture

Located in Dongguan, China, the Vanke Architecture Research Center (VARC) focuses on studies related to the housing industry. It is the research base of special architectural materials, low energy-consumption methodologies, and eco-landscape studies. The focus of eco-landscape study is the development of environmentally friendly materials, such as the application of precast concrete modules in future real-estate projects, the exploration of different types of pervious materials, and plant selection and arrangement.

In order to achieve the goal of low maintenance overall on campus, two major issues had to be addressed: stormwater management, and low-maintenance construction and planting materials.

To control runoff, two small triangular sites were designed as 'ripple gardens'. The canopy tree is the most efficient element in stormwater management because of its prolonged rainwater dripping period. The slope of the lawn and the wave can be adjusted for increased infiltration, without triggering water-logging or speedy flow. The space between the waves uses different pervious materials (the bark, the ceramics, the gravel and sand). The edge of the waves is designed to allow observation and comparison of the overflow amount of different materials.

To control the stormwater, the 'windmill garden' has a 105-foot (32-meter) windmill that provides power for pumping the collected stormwater to the building roof for oxygen exposure. The primary purification is not finished until the water falls down to the retention pool. Then, the stormwater passes a series of phytoremediation pools. The purified stormwater flows through an examination valve. The standardized purified water enters a reflection pool, serving as a playing space for children. The remaining water returns to the cycling system for another round of purification.

Precast concrete (PC) technique is well developed and widely used in the US and EU countries. In terms of appearance, the size, color, and texture of PC modules are similar to granite, but it has a significant effect on reducing energy consumption.

First, the replacement of granite with PC avoids extra mining. Second, paving areas in some countries require a concrete support slab, which means rainwater cannot penetrate where there is pavement. PC is so thick that the concrete slab can be removed, and the rainwater is able to penetrate the ground. Meanwhile, PC can be customized to enable a grass-embedded pavement. It can improve the visual effects and eco-friendliness of large pavement areas stipulated by regulations, such as parking lots and fire lanes. It can also be used for various outdoor structures, such as benches and bike racks. With the help of molds, the appearance can be customized, and endurance can be improved, allowing wider use in future housing projects in many regions.

Location |
Dongguan, China
Completion date |
2012
Site area |
7.3acres (3 hectares)
Landscape design |
Z+T Studio
Client |
Vanke Architecture Research Center (VARC)
Photography |
Hai Zhang

1 | 2
3 | 4

1. Precast concrete steps
2. Corner of Ripple Garden I
3. Channel of Ripple Garden I
4. Ripple Garden II

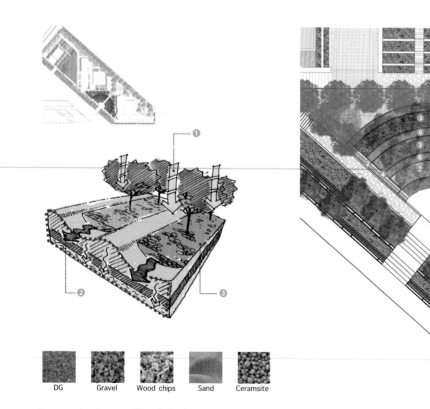

DG Gravel Wood chips Sand Ceramsite

① Rainfall
② Overflow
③ Porous material
④ Retaining wall
⑤ Observing terrace
⑥ Landform

Cross-section drawing of Ripple Garden I

Plan of Ripple Garden I

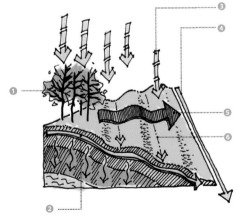

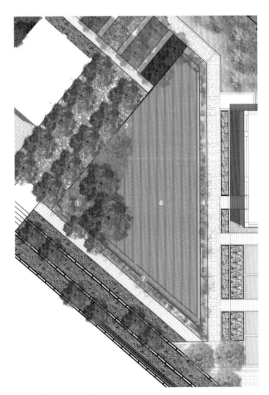

① Canopy tree
② Maximize infiltration
③ Rainfall
④ Bioswale
⑤ 50 percent slope
⑥ 2 percent slope
⑦ Retaining wall
⑧ Rolling field

Cross-section drawing of Ripple Garden II

Plan of Ripple Garden II

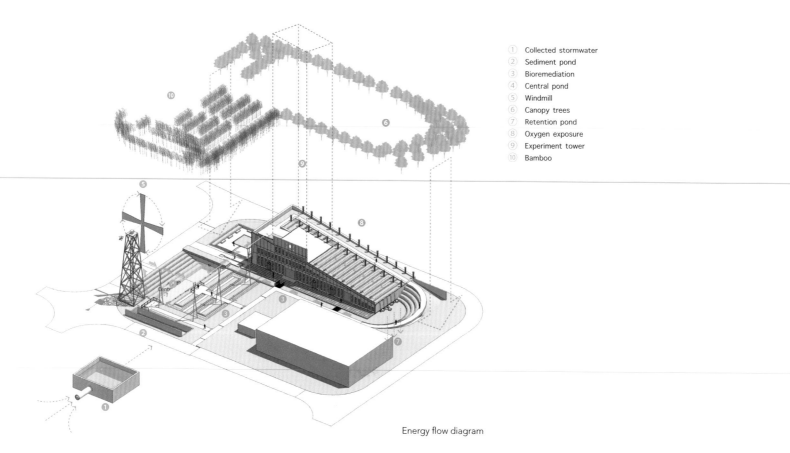

1. Collected stormwater
2. Sediment pond
3. Bioremediation
4. Central pond
5. Windmill
6. Canopy trees
7. Retention pond
8. Oxygen exposure
9. Experiment tower
10. Bamboo

Energy flow diagram

1. Rain garden and windmill in the background
2. Specially designed precast concrete paving
3. Rain garden
4. Precast concrete bike rack

$$\frac{1}{2}\begin{array}{|c|}3\\\hline4\end{array}$$

1. Bird's-eye view to the windmill garden
2. Diagram of cascading wetland
3. Plants in windmill garden
4. Wild grass gracefully integrates with the precast paving

4 | Solar Photovoltaic Power-generation Technology

The photovoltaic power-generation system is a technology that turns luminous energy into electric energy by taking advantage of the photovoltaic effect of semiconductor interfaces. The key device of this technology is solar cells. Solar cells connected in series and wrapped safely can form big areas of solar-cell modules. With parts like power controllers, they become a photovoltaic power-generation device. The merit of a photovoltaic power-generation system is that it is subject to fewer geographic restrictions; at the same time, it has the virtues of being safe and reliable, free of noises, and with low pollution and no consumption of fuels.

Elements of solar photovoltaic power-generation systems

The solar photovoltaic power generation system consists of solar panels, solar controllers, and storage batteries (packs).

Solar panels

Solar panels are the core and most valuable parts of a solar-power system. Its function is to transform solar power into electric power, store solar power in the storage battery, or activate loading operation. The quality and cost of solar panels can directly affect the quality and cost of the whole system.

Solar controller

A solar controller is responsible for controlling the operating status of the whole system and protecting storage batteries against overcharge and overdischarge. In areas with big temperature differences, qualified controllers have the function of compensating for temperature. Other attached functions such as photo switching and time switching are optional for controllers.

Storage batteries

Storage batteries are often lead-acid batteries and are available in 12 volts and 24 volts. For microsystems, nickel-metal hydride batteries, nickel-cadmium batteries, or lithium batteries can be used. The function of storage batteries is to store the electric power emitted by solar panels when there is sunlight, and release it when necessary.

Inverter

In many occasions, AC power of 220 volts or 110 volts is needed. As the direct output of solar power is often in DC as 12 volts, 24 volts or 48 volts, for the purpose of supplying power to AC 220 volt electric appliances, we need to transform the DC power generated by the solar power-generation system into AC power. Therefore, DC–AC inverters are needed. When loads of varied voltages are required, DC–AC inverters are also needed, for example, to change 24 volt DC power into 5 volt DC power (note that it is not a simple reduction of voltage).

Classification of solar photovoltaic power-generation systems

As per requirements of different situations, solar photovoltaic power-generation systems can be generally classified into three types: independent-power-supply, solar photovoltaic power-generation systems; grid-connected solar photovoltaic power-generation systems; and hybrid solar photovoltaic power-generation systems.

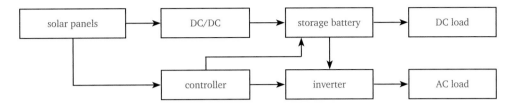

Diagram 11: Structure diagram of independent-power-supply, solar photovoltaic power-generation systems

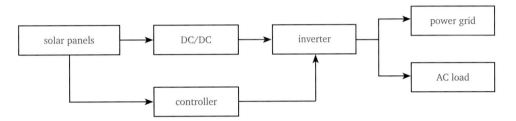

Diagram 12: Structural diagram of a grid-connected solar photovoltaic system

Independent-power-supply, solar photovoltaic power-generation systems

The independent-power-supply, solar photovoltaic power-generation system is shown in diagram 11. The whole system is comprised of solar panels, storage batteries, controllers, and inverters. Solar panels, as the core part of the system, can directly turn solar power into DC electric power and usually output power only in the daytime. As per demands of load, the system often chooses lead-acid batteries as the energy storage device. When generated energy exceeds load, solar panels can charge storage batteries through chargers. When the generated energy is insufficient, solar panels and storage batteries can supply extra power. The controller normally consists of charging circuits, discharging circuits, and follow-up control of maximum power points. The function of inverters is to directly transform DC power into AC power with the same phase of AC load.

Grid-connected solar photovoltaic power-generation systems

The grid-connected solar photovoltaic power-generation system is shown in diagram 12. It is directly connected with the power grid, in which the inverter plays an important role and is required to have the capability to join in the power grid. Currently, the most frequently used grid-connected solar photovoltaic system has two structural forms that differ in whether they have storage batteries as an energy storage link. The grid-connected solar photovoltaic system with storage batteries is generally called an adjustable grid-connected solar photovoltaic system. As this system is equipped with master switches and major load switches, it has the same functions of uninterrupted power supply (UPS), which for some domestic users is quite significant. This system could also function as a power regulator to stabilize the grid voltage and counteract harmful ultra-harmonics components so as to improve quality of electric energy. The grid-connected solar photovoltaic system without storage batteries is called a non-adjustable grid-connected solar photovoltaic system. In this system, the grid-connected inverter can directly transform DC power produced by solar panels into AC power at the same frequency and phase with the power grid. When the main power grid is cutoff, the system will automatically cease power supply to the power grid. When there is sunlight and the AC power generated by the photovoltaic system surpasses the amount required, the excess energy will be transmitted to the power grid; when the power needed exceeds the AC power generated by the photovoltaic system during the night, the power grid will automatically provide supplement energy.

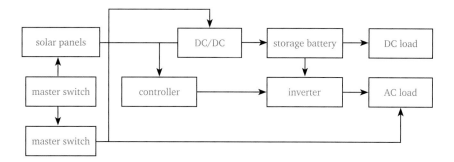

Diagram 13: Structural diagram of a hybrid solar photovoltaic power-generation system

Hybrid solar photovoltaic power-generation systems

The hybrid solar photovoltaic power-generation system is shown in diagram 13. Its main difference from the previously discussed two systems is that it has a standby generating set. When the power generated by the photovoltaic array or the storage energy of the batteries is insufficient, it not only can directly supply power to the AC load, but also can charge batteries through a current rectifier; therefore, it is called a hybrid solar photovoltaic power-generation system.

Design of hybrid solar photovoltaic power-generation systems

The design of solar photovoltaic power-generation systems shall take the following factors into account:

1. Where shall the solar photovoltaic system be used? What is the availability of sunlight there?

2. How much is the power load of the system?

3. How much is the output voltage of the system? Is it DC power or AC power?

4. How many hours does the system need to work for?

5. Under rainy and cloudy when there is no sunshine, for how many days shall the system need to supply power?

6. What's the load? Is it pure resistive, capacitive, or inductive? How much is the start-up current?

7. What's the demand of the system?

General design principles of solar photovoltaic systems

The design of solar photovoltaic systems can be classified into soft design and hard design, with priority given to the former. The soft design mainly includes calculation of power consumption of load, calculation of the radiation of the solar panel matrix, calculation of the consumption of solar panels and storage batteries as well as optimization design of mutual matching of them, calculation of the installation angle of the solar panel matrix, prediction of the system's operation state and analysis of the system's economic efficiency. The hard design primarily covers the selection of load forms and necessary designs, model selection of solar panels and storage batteries, design of solar panel supports, model selection and design of inverters, and design of control and measuring systems. As for large-scale solar photovoltaic systems, there still are designs for the array field of photovoltaic panels and lighting protection.

As the soft design involves complicated design calculations of the solar radiation amount, installation angle, and optimization of system, it is usually done by a computer. When the requirements are less strict, estimations can be used in the design.

The general principle of solar photovoltaic system design, under the condition of satisfying the demand of full-load power supply, is to use minimum power of the solar panel set and minimum capacity of the storage batteries so as to minimize initial investment. For any improper choices, the cost to the system is greatly increased and may not meet the requirements for use. After making the decision to build an independent solar photovoltaic system, the design could be carried out according to the followings steps: calculate the load, select the capacity of storage batteries and solar panel matrix, choose controllers and inverters, and finally consider hybrid power generation.

Prior to the design of a solar photovoltaic system, it is necessary to learn and acquire some basic data for calculations: site geographical location of the photovoltaic system, including its location, latitude, longitude, and elevation; meteorological data of the region such as monthly total solar radiation, direction radiation and scattering radiation; yearly average temperature, maximum and minimum air temperature, longest period of continually rainy and cloudy weather, maximum wind speed, and less common weather such as hail and snow.

Calculation of capacity of solar photovoltaic systems

The major purpose of capacity design is to calculate the number of solar panel sets and storage batteries needed for reliable operation of the system in one year. Meanwhile, the relation between maximum reliability and the operating cost of the system must be balanced. It shall offer reliable performance while reducing the cost as much as possible.

Design of storage batteries

The design idea of storage batteries is to ensure normal operation of the system when the sunshine is consistently lower than average. When designing storage batteries, we need to work on an indispensable parameter, such as number of self-sufficient days. This parameter enables the system designer to decide the required capacity of storage batteries.

Generally, the determination of self-sufficient days is related to two factors: the demand of load for power and the meteorological conditions of the installation site of the photovoltaic system. Normally, the maximum duration of continually rainy and cloudy days at the site of the system could be used as the number of self-sufficient days in the design of the system; however, the demand of load for power shall also be taken into overall consideration. When the requirements of power load are less strict in the application of the photovoltaic system, the number of self-sufficient days is taken as three to five days. The so-called system with loose load restrictions means that users can slightly adjust the load demand to adapt it to the inconveniences brought about by bad weather. In strict systems, the power load is important, such as in communication, navigation, or other important health facilities such as hospitals and clinics. Moreover, the location of the photovoltaic system shall also be considered. If it is located in a remote area, storage batteries with large capacity shall be designed, as it takes longer for the maintenance staff to arrive at the site.

Holland Eco Garden Xi'an

Creating the Dutch garden for Xi'an's Garden Show in 2011 offered the opportunity to present innovative ideas within society in a miniature landscape. OKRA's interests lie in studying today's challenges presented within the delta landscape, and researching an integrated solution to climate change and rising sea levels, in combination with urban expansion. Water management in the landscape needs to be retained and filtered within the city boundaries.

The garden designed by OKRA is more than just a controlled landscape; it represents the contemporary relationship between humankind and nature. It focuses on the symbiosis between consumption and production, between dynamic and rest. The eco-garden represents the idea that future urban green spaces will be linked to sustainable water management, a healthy energy cycle, and recycling resources, waste, and nutrients. The garden generates energy and focuses upon creating public awareness about water management and water systems.

Innovative cultivation techniques were implemented to demonstrate the possibilities of sustainable urban farming. Production of plants requires linking the cycle of nutrients to the water and energy cycles. The sustainable technology of the garden is closely related to life cycles within an artificial system, thus creating harmony with nature and offering an exceptional experience of a working landscape.

Location |
Xi'an, China
Completion date |
2011
Area |
21,527 square feet (2000 square meters)
Landscape design |
OKRA: Martin Knuit, Eva Radionova
TektonArchitekten: Bert Tjhie, ThysSchrei

Eusino: Tao Wang, Mariska Stevens
Archipelontwerpers: Eric
Vreedenburgh, Guido Zeck
Client |
Xian International Horticultural
Exposition 2011 Xian
Photography |
OKRA

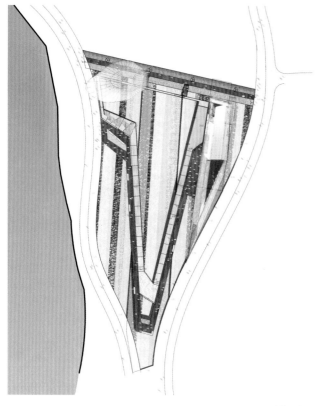

Site plan

Pavilion plants

1. View of terrace to vistas of the landscape
2. Environmental process and constant flow of water around continuous pavilion path

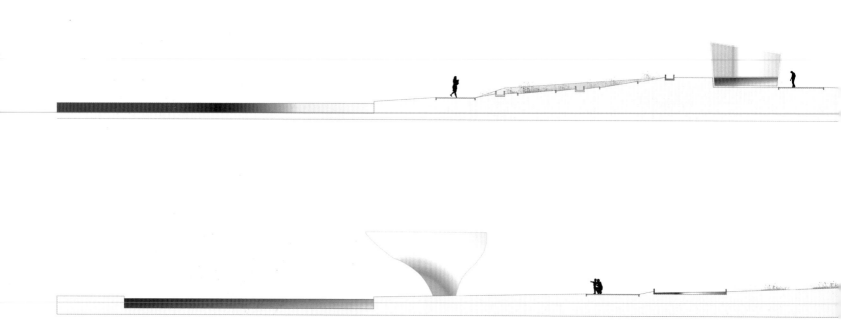

Cross-section plan of the Eco Garden

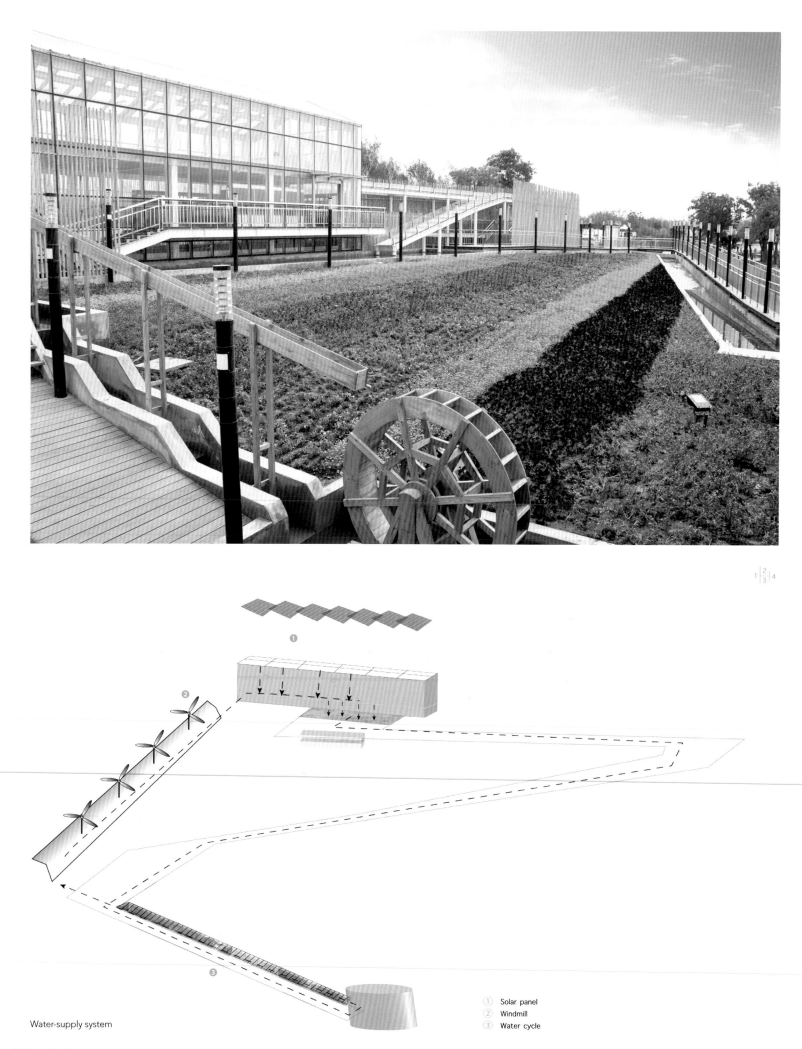

1 | 2/3 | 4

Water-supply system

① Solar panel
② Windmill
③ Water cycle

Rendering of water cycle

1. Dutch polder landscape and the colorful flower cultivation
2. Water from high level to low level
3. Water ditches in the high level
4. Stairs in the pavilion

1. Landscape harmonizing with architecture
2. Panorama
3. Corner view of water cycle and garden
4. Beautiful flowers in the garden

Cross-section

George 'Doc' Cavalliere Park

Almost 25 years in the making, Cavalliere Park is a product of not only extensive community input, but also the significant challenges of integrating a community park into a regional stormwater retention facility, set into the rugged desert terrain of north Scottsdale. The resulting project has established a new standard for the design and implementation of a truly sustainable community park for the City of Scottsdale.

Preserving open space, respecting existing neighborhoods, and creating a demonstration project for sustainability were the primary guiding principles in the design of George 'Doc' Cavalliere Park. Almost two-thirds of the total park was preserved as a permanent natural open area. High-efficiency LED lighting was used throughout the site and a 24,800 kilowatt hour solar photovoltaic system provides 100 percent of the park's energy requirements, resulting in net-zero energy consumption. The native landscape palette, in conjunction with the rainwater harvesting system, enables the landscape to thrive without supplemental irrigation.

The project utilizes a 100 percent native plant palette. A number of beautiful existing mesquite trees, that were too large to salvage, were incorporated into the layout of the parking and shade structure. All other trees and cacti were salvaged and used to restore significant areas of Sonoran upland and riparian plant communities. Parking, driveways, and paths were paved with stabilized decomposed granite, which utilized site-salvaged materials and dramatically reduced drainage runoff and the urban heat island effect, while retaining the natural desert character.

Steel, concrete, and rock-filled gabions provide a regionally appropriate and sustainable material palette. All site elements were custom designed and locally produced using either natural steel or concrete. The natural steel roof panels, structural components, planters, bridge, and other site elements are all made from high-percentage content recycled steel and continue the palette of desert colors and textures found in the paving and gabion structures. The strict use of natural unfinished materials eliminated the on-site release of VOC (volatile organic compounds) and will greatly reduce future maintenance and environmental costs. Even details such as the lines on the basketball court, which are sandblasted instead of painted, contribute to the sustainable goals of the project.

A large open wildflower field/play area was designed as an elevated plinth that can be utilized even when the retention basin is inundated with water. A second play area is set on a slope and utilizes an artificial turf system made from 100 percent recycled plastic. In response to neighborhood concerns, the lit sport courts were terraced into the side of the existing topography to lower their elevation, thereby reducing their visibility to the existing homes. The shape and design of the central canopy and restrooms took their form directly from the nature of the site, with the roof shape closely mirroring the slope and tilt of the adjacent mountainside, and the restroom walls utilizing the same gabion construction as the site's retaining walls. In addition to providing shade, the canopy roof also functions as a large rainwater collection area, which directs water into a central collection basin, where it is then distributed to the native landscape.

Location |

Scottsdale, Arizona, United States

Completion date |

2012

Area |

34 acres (13.76 hectares)

Landscape design |

Floor Associates

Client |

City of Scottsdale

Photography |

Bill Timmerman and Chris Brown

Cavalliere Park has established a new benchmark for sustainable practices, demonstrating how to appropriately design and construct an active community park in a sensitive desert context. It is well used and highly appreciated by residents and visitors, making a significant contribution to the quality of life of the community.

1. 20-foot-high (6.1-meter-high) steel 'focal walls' were carefully placed to provide a dramatic sculptural element at the pavilion portal, with the three windows converging to frame the distant granite pinnacle.
2. The design successfully blurs the lines between the built and natural environments to create a beautiful modern expression, nestled into a dramatic Sonoran Desert site

1. Artificial turf
2. Wildflower plinth
3. Covered playground
4. Restrooms
5. Basketball court
6. Hiking trails
7. Parking
8. Sunrise terrace
9. Gabion 'window wall'
10. Steel focal walls
11. Vista shelters

The design team worked closely with the adjacent neighborhoods, hydrologists and the city team to integrate the park and nearly 50 acre-feet (61,670 cubic meters) of stormwater retention into the rugged desert site.

1. The strong converging lines of the structures and landscape are reinforced by the interplay of light and shadows
2. Naturally weathered steel retaining walls were used to maintain the bosque of existing native mesquite trees in place, creating a beautiful 'parking garden'

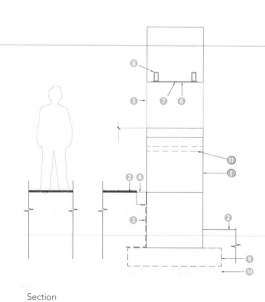

Bench and table

①	CIP concrete bench
②	Back of bench
③	CIP concrete table
④	4 inches (101.6 millimeters) reveal on all sides
⑤	Stabilized decomposed granite

Section

Elevation

①	Gabion wall
②	Finish grade of turf
③	Filter fabric
④	Turf edge
⑤	Gabion opening
⑥	Steel plate lintel natural finish
⑦	1-inch (25.4-millimeter) diameter drain hole
⑧	TS beam welded to lintel plate
⑨	CIP concrete footing
⑩	Compacted subgrade
⑪	3-inch (76.2-millimeter) ODSS pipe penetration, insert into 3 x 3 inches (76.2 x 76.2 millimeters) of gabion basket mesh

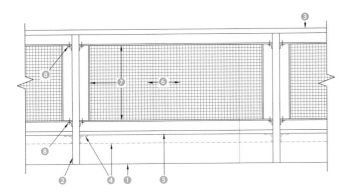

Bridge typical elevation

1. Tube steel ridge beam
2. Tube steel rail post welded to beam
3. Steel channel handrail welded to rail post
4. Angle iron to support grating behind beam, welded to beam
5. Steel bar grating
6. 2 x 2 inches (50.8 x 50.8 millimeters) McNichols weld-mesh GA.156. welded to framing
7. Steel bar frame for weld-mesh panel
8. Angle iron welded to rail post

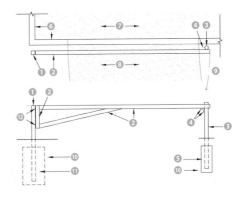

Vehicular swing gate

1. 4 x 4 inches (101.6 x 101.6 millimeters) of tube steel post, natural finish
2. 2 x 2 inches (50.8 x 50.8 millimeters) of tube steel natural finish
3. Steel-pipe natural-finish gate stopper at opening position and closing position
4. 3 inches (76.2 millimeters) in diameter, 0.5-inch-thick (12.7-millimeter-thick) steel ring, cut and weld to gate and gate stoppers
5. 12 inches (304.8 millimeters) in diameter CIP concrete footing
6. Concrete curb
7. Asphalt parking of fire station
8. Maintenance access drive
9. Landscape area
10. Compacted subgrade
11. 24 inches (609.6 millimeters) in diameter CIP concrete footing
12. Stainless steel hinges

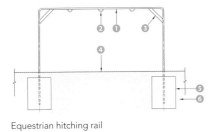

Equestrian hitching rail

1. #11 rebar
2. 3 inches (76.2 millimeters) in diameter steel ring, cut and weld to steel rebar
3. 2 x 3/8 inches (50.8 x 9.5 millimeters) of steel flat bar welded to rebar
4. Compacted soil, compact to 90 percent to min. depth of 6 inches (152.4 millimeters)
5. 18 inches (457.2 millimeters) in diameter CIP concrete footing
6. Compacted subgrade

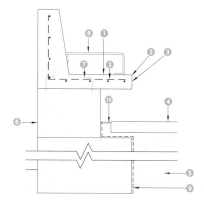

1. Precast concrete seat back, smooth finish
2. 0.5 inch (12.7 millimeters) chamfer on edges
3. Refer to 101 / S-301 for reinforcement
4. Finish grade of concrete paving
5. 95 percent compacted subgrade
6. Gabion retaining wall
7. Anchor, welded to gabion basket, refer to 101 / S-301
8. 3 x 3/8 inch (76.2 x 9.5 millimeter) steel flat bar armrest
9. Filter fabric
10. Stabilized DG

Precast concrete seat on gabion back

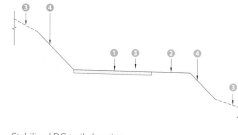

Stabilized DG trail elevation

1. Stabilized DG trail
2. Compacted soil equestrian trail
3. Existing hill slope
4. Graded hill slope

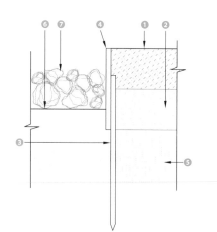

1. Stabilized DG
2. Compacted aggregate base course, refer to H-401 for thickness
3. 0.5 inch (12.7 millimeters) in diameter steel rod
4. 3/8-inch-thick (9.5-millimeter-thick) mild steel plate, natural finish
5. Compacted subgrade
6. Finish grade of landscape area
7. Desert cobble riprap

Edge of stabilized DG

Swale section with steel edge

1. Ungrouted riprap rock cobble
2. Stabilized DG where occurs
3. Steel header
4. 95 percent compacted subgrade
5. Landscape area
6. Filter fabric

1. Soaring steel pavilion appears to float above the central playground to provide critical shade and comfort to this Sonoran Desert park
2. Each panel of the 'focal walls' was set at a different height and the windows are precisely offset, so that the framed view is orchestrated to occur only at a specific location at the center of the space, aligning the view with the granite pinnacle and the rising sun
3. Natural unfinished materials were used throughout to eliminate the on-site release of harmful VOC's and to minimize ongoing maintenance. Instead of paint, the lines on the basketball court were permanently sandblasted in place

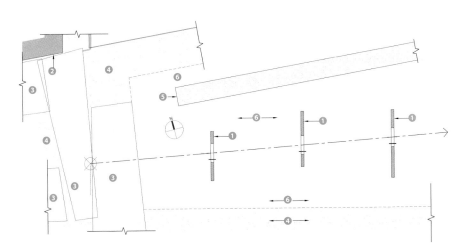

Steel focal walls layout

① Steel focal wall
② Gabion wall of restroom
③ Concrete paving
④ Stabilized DG
⑤ Gabion wall
⑥ Landscape area

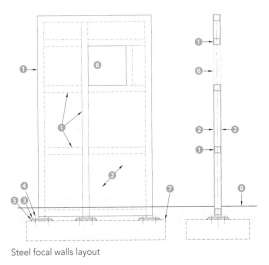

Steel focal walls layout

① 6 X 6 TS wall frame natural finish
② Steel plate natural finish welded to steel frame
③ Steel base plate
④ Anchor bolt
⑤ Nonshrink grout
⑥ Focal window opening
⑦ CIP concrete foundation
⑧ Finish grade

1. Precast concrete shelf, natural gray, medium sandblast finish, weld to steel pipe, 0.25-inch (6.4-millimeter) radius at all corners
2. 3 inches (76.2 millimeters) in diameter steel pipe
3. 2 inches (50.8 millimeters) in diameter steel pipe foot rest, weld to steel rod
4. 1-inch (25.4-millimeter) steel rod support
5. #4 rebar 6 inches (152.4 millimeters) in length each way
6. 9 inches (228.6 millimeters) in diameter CIP concrete footing
7. Gabion basket
8. Filter fabric
9. Stabilized terrace
10. Basin
11. 95 percent compacted subgrade

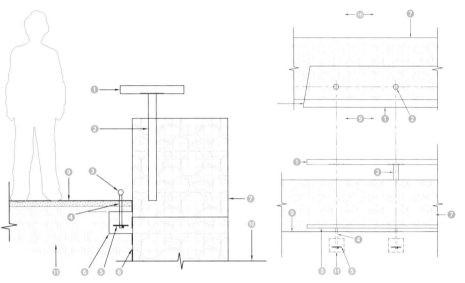

Precast concrete shelf and foot rest

1. All site elements were custom fabricated from cast in place concrete and or unfinished steel, including the 'Sunrise Terrace' pictured here
2. The design responds beautifully to the site and the Sonoran Desert environment. It is one of the best examples of an integrated modern approach to sustainable open space design in the southwest and was the first SITE-certified project in Arizona
3. Native rock was skillfully placed into custom gabions to form the buildings and site structures, including the freestanding Window Wall. More than 4000 rock-filled gabions were used to blend into and to celebrate the inherent beauty of the site's rugged desert typology

1. Shelf
2. Foot rest
3. Gabion wall
4. Light fixture
5. Stabilized DG

Terrace gabion wall elevation, north

Bestseller Office Complex

The new office complex for about 800 employees of Bestseller is intended as a showroom for Bestseller's design-driven corporate identity, and resembles a varied flotilla of buildings at different levels, which are connected by a series of outdoor atria, courtyards, terraces, and roof gardens.

The mixture of office buildings and outdoor spaces creates the impression that this is a town within a town. The complex, surrounded by canals and lakes on all four sides, forms the entrance to the new, urban district on the waterfront in Aarhus, Denmark.

The office complex uses seawater cooling and solar energy, and is planned as a low-energy-class building (i.e. energy consumption will be 50 percent lower than the minimum requirements stated in the building regulations).

The focal point of the complex is an internal 'street' with a central indoor plaza laid over a road passage, which splits the building's ground floor into two halves. From the plaza, there is access to a communal auditorium, meeting facilities, and experimental store environments. Somewhere between 500 and 1000 people can gather on the plateau, stairs, and balconies to attend large fashion shows and meetings.

The entrance is shaped like a bridge, from which there are views of the building's three underground levels. From the internal street there are varying glimpses into the outer green terraces and rooftop gardens—10 green outdoor spaces in all. The street leads to the restaurant area, which is subdivided into many sections with different ambiences, sizes, and degrees of privacy, from where there is direct access to terraces and a brand-new canal.

The atriums, terraces, and rooftop gardens serve as green islands between the building volumes. The exquisitely detailed rooftop gardens feature thematic use of grasses, ferns, mosses, and elegant trees with sparse leaves to create a variety of different atmospheres. Rainwater is collected and reused for watering the gardens.

The outdoor areas around Bestseller's office complex merge seamlessly with the public space on the Aarhus waterfront. The granite of the car park and the cobblestones of the square interact naturally with the new district's materials.

Location |
Port of Aarhus, Denmark
Completion date |
2015
Site area |
5.44 acres (2.2 hectares)
Landscape design |
C.F. Møller Landscape

Client |
Bestseller A/S
Photography |
C.F. Møller Landscape
Awards |
Aarhus Municipality Architecture
Award 2015, WAN Commercial of
the Year Award 2015

1. Bestseller's office complex is a landmark in the new urban district along the Aarhus Harbour waterfront.
2. The complex, surrounded by canals and lakes on all four sides, forms the entrance to the new, urban district on the waterfront in Aarhus
3. Panoramic views from the terraces contrast with the more sheltered garden spaces
4. Extensions of the façade openings form sheltering colonnades along the north and south gardens
5. Bestseller also makes use of the outdoor spaces for public events like fashion shows or sports.

1 | 2 | 3
4 | 5

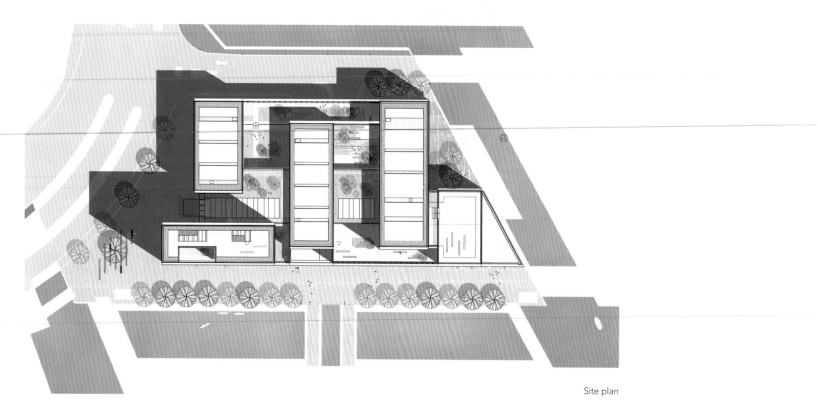

Site plan

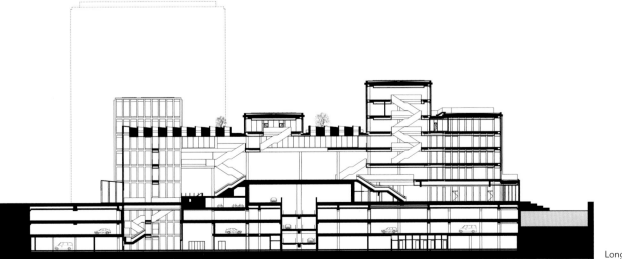

Longitudinal section

1. The exquisitely detailed rooftop gardens feature thematic use of grasses, ferns, mosses and elegant trees with sparse leaves to create a variety of different atmospheres
2. From the restaurant there is direct access to terraces and a brand-new canal across the erstwhile Pier 2
3. Ten green outdoor spaces are distributed across the various levels of the complex

1 | 2 | 3

Energy-efficient solutions such as seawater cooling systems and solar cells ensure that the building meets the requirements for low-energy-class 2015

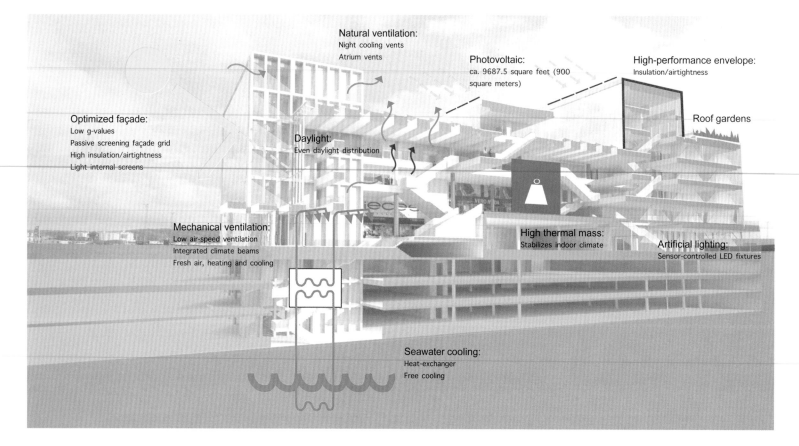

Natural ventilation:
Night cooling vents
Atrium vents

Photovoltaic:
ca. 9687.5 square feet (900 square meters)

High-performance envelope:
Insulation/airtightness

Optimized façade:
Low g-values
Passive screening façade grid
High insulation/airtightness
Light internal screens

Daylight:
Even daylight distribution

Roof gardens

Mechanical ventilation:
Low air-speed ventilation
Integrated climate beams
Fresh air, heating and cooling

High thermal mass:
Stabilizes indoor climate

Artificial lighting:
Sensor-controlled LED fixtures

Seawater cooling:
Heat-exchanger
Free cooling

5 | Rainwater Recycling and other Rainwater Management Technologies

The purpose of recycling rainwater is to reduce water usage. Rainwater recycling not only covers rainwater collection and water saving, but also contributes to reducing rainwater logging, reducing use of underground water, controlling source pollution, and improving the environment. This section describes in detail the role of landscaping in filtration and recycling of rainwater, and discusses the feasibility of rainwater collection and methods of collection and recycling. It will also introduce some other common energy-saving rainwater management technologies.

Main collection methods of rainwater

Recessed greenbelts

Recessed greenbelts play a significant role in rainwater collection. They can increase holding time of rainwater in greenbelts. On one hand, they can enhance rainwater storage and infiltration capacity of soil, save water for landscaping, and increase the amount of underground water; on the other hand, they can put into full use the soil's sewage intercepting and infiltration capability of water so as to improve the quality of infiltrated rainwater and the environment of underground water. Through reasonable designs of terrain, rainwater outlets are placed inside the greenbelts (above the level of greenbelts but below the level of road surface), thus only when the greenbelt is saturated can rainwater flow into the outlets. Then rainwater runoff from roads, buildings, and pavements is forced to go first into the greenbelts where the plant roots can be fully utilized to purify suspended solids and impurities in the rainwater. The quality of rainwater is thus improved. Moreover, greenbelts have high capacity of infiltration; therefore they can make up for the imbalance between rainfall and water infiltration. They can also cut down runoff and peak discharge. In case of heavy rain, the plant roots can enhance the water retention and flood reduction effect of recessed greenbelts.

Pavement and structures with water permeability

The expansion of hard pavement has brought adverse effects to the ecological environment, including city landscape and rainwater runoff. Wide application and reasonable choice of pavement materials with water permeability in landscaping

Sunshine Cove: Recessed greenbelt

Novo Nordisk Nature Park: Water permeability of pavement

design can facilitate infiltration of rainwater, further contain continual decline of underground water level, improve the environment of underground water, and upgrade the design of the site. Pavement materials with water permeability work well in collecting water and recharging underground water. When it rains, permeable materials allow rainwater to infiltrate underground, increase underground water volume, adjust air humidity, and purify air. This is especially important in water-deficient areas. What is also worth mentioning is the permeable ceramic brick, which has high strength and good slip-proof performance. It can be used in parking lots, sidewalks, and pedestrian areas. Permeable bituminous pavement has a permeable rate of 59 inches (1500 millimeters) per hour, 60 times that of common clay. Its service life is 5 years longer than that of traditional bituminous pavement, and all of its properties are better than those of the latter. Furthermore, it is not more expensive.

Landscaping water features

Other than a beautiful and unique water feature, landscaping water features with a good structural design can also collect rainwater, sometimes with a capacity large enough to cope with flood season. With proper purification treatment, they can not only meet the water demands of landscaping, but also can be used for irrigation of landscaping vegetation and road cleaning. Therefore, they can effectively reduce consumption of water for landscaping, and even can achieve zero discharge of landscaping rainfall, improve city environment, increase the total volume of water resources, and relieve the crisis of city water resources. In landscaping areas with large quantities of soft and permeable underlying surface, the landscaping water feature, with its natural regulation and storage function, can regulate and store natural rainwater. Landscaping design can take full advantage of water features such as fountains, creeks, rivers, and artificial lakes, and proper water-supply facilities to store rainwater runoff.

Landscaping rainwater recycling and reusing system

Rainwater collection and storage pools, crushed stone canals and ditches, grass-planted shallow gullies, and sand-bed infiltration systems can be used for collection of rainwater from road surfaces, roofs, sites, and greenbelts. The whole process of rainwater collection, infiltration, and reuse forms a highly efficient and organic system.

After the treatment of sedimentation, infiltration, adsorption, and sterilization, the quality of collected and stored rainwater can almost meet the quality standard of water for the use of landscaping. It can be put to uses such as supplementing landscaping lakes and fountains as well as vehicle cleaning, which have high requirements for water quality. The spillovers of collection and storage pools are directly discharged into municipal rainwater pipes. Tap-water supplement inlets are reserved for landscaping lake and fountain features for the convenience of regulation and management. The rainwater collection and reuse system shown in the diagram 14 collects and reuses rainwater from road surfaces, roofs, sites, and

greenbelts by optimal methods. This system not only fully utilizes water resources, but also saves them and is very important for sustainable development of the environment.

The rainwater collection and infiltration mechanism of landscaping mainly consists of three parts: grassed shallow gullies, infiltration crushed stone canals and ditches, and sand-bed infiltration systems. The grassed shallow gullies are surface canals and ditches planted with herbage. When rainwater runs off through it, the pollutants in them can be reduced by the absorption of plants and biodegradation process, and thus achieve the purpose of rainwater collection and reuse as well as containment of runoff pollution. In the design of grassed shallow gullies, the designers generally give full consideration to the gullies' ability to purify rainwater. The surface of shallow gullies can be planted with zoysia japonica, bermuda grass and other herbage to collect most runoff from greenbelts and non-permeable roads in landscaping, and directly guide them into rainstorm pools for temporary storage.

Diagram14: Landscaping rainwater collection and reuse system

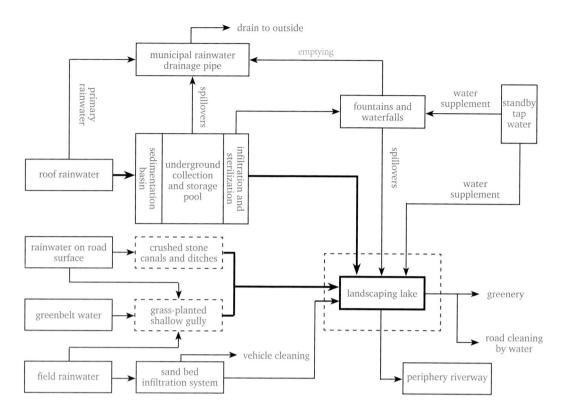

Infiltration crushed stone canals and ditches refer to low-lying areas of the surrounding water-catchment area. It is a linear basin with crushed stones of various sizes as the main structure. After overland runoff enters the crushed canals and ditches in the water-catchment area, they infiltrate underground through a crushed stone layer. After infiltration and degradation by the physical structure of crushed stones and grown biological membranes, the water has been purified and finally becomes the supplementary water resource for the lake.

A sand-bed infiltration system is composed of rainwater pools, infiltration sand beds, and water-collecting wells. It is a rainwater collecting system chiefly relying on fine-sand infiltration. To decrease the erosion effect of overland runoff, and to remove particles in them, the rainwater pools shall be at least 31.5 inches (80 centimeters) deep. After infiltrating the sand beds, the overland runoff will flow into water-collecting wells. The system's purification effect of water is clearly better than shallow gullies with plants or crushed stones.

A rainwater natural infiltration system refers to organized natural infiltration of rainwater by greenbelts and soil. It can supplement underground water and is an important part of ecological landscaping. It primarily takes the forms of landscaping water, and storage and infiltration pools. This system plays an important part in sustainable development. It can not only cut down

rainwater runoff, lower cost of constructing rain piping networks, and reduce water pollution; it can also optimize the structure of underground soil and effectively supplement underground water. The rainwater natural infiltration system can be applied in a variety of forms. It can use roadside ditches, greenbelts or green pools, and infiltration pavements in combination with rain piping network to collect, infiltrate, and discharge rainwater. Rainwater can naturally infiltrate underground through road greenbelts or green pools. It can flow into recessed areas in greenbelts and green pools by rainwater outlets. When the recessed areas are filled with rainwater, the overflow will enter the rain piping system by placing outlets at the edges of the recessed area. The collected water in greenbelts and green pools naturally infiltrates deep into the soil and supplements underground water.

To sum up, rainwater recycling and reuse mainly refers to reuse, collection and infiltration, and slow discharge of rainwater. It can be divided into two components according to their purposes. The first component is to retain water in water-collecting containers. The rainwater, after being treated by processing facilities, can be used as irrigation water and road-cleaning water. The second component is that through organized natural infiltration by greenbelts and soil, the rainwater can supplement underground water (see diagram 14).

Other rainwater management technologies

Vegetation filter strips

Vegetation filter strips are usually covered with vegetation (mainly turf). Usually their converging surfaces are level and constructed in relatively flat areas. They are used to collect large areas of scattering laminar flow intercepted by upper-stream converging surfaces. It could also be used to process runoff from small areas such as streets, expressways, and parking lots. According to the design approaches and functions, vegetation filter strips could be classified into many types, such as grass filter strips, buffer strips, waterfront vegetation buffer strips, and artificial filter strips.

With vegetation filter strips, pollutants can be removed through interception and filtration of vegetation as well as permeation and adsorption of soil. The strip's major functions are as following:

- effectively intercept and reduce suspending solid particles and organic pollutants;
- protect soil against erosion in rainstorms to decrease water and soil loss
- use as a pretreatment measure for rainwater follow-up processing. When adopted in combination with other rainwater management technologies, it could cut down the maintenance cost, extend the system's life and improve its capabilities
- be connected with non-permeable areas or other technological measures and create relatively good landscaping effects.

Bioretention facilities

Building Bioretention facilities is an effective rainwater purification and treatment technology. Usually built in low-lying areas, it can purify and absorb small areas of converged initial rainwater through natural soil or altered artificial soil and plants. Bioretention facilities have low construction costs, and are easy to operate and manage. At the same time, they are natural and beautiful and can be perfectly integrated with landscaping.

The major parts of a bioretention facility include an aquifer, a bark covering layer, plants, planting soil, a packing layer, and a gravel layer. If there are requirements for water recycling or discharging, catchment and perforated pipes can be embedded in the gravel layer. A sand layer or a fine gravel layer can be used to protect pipes against being blocked by particle matter. Bioretention facilities could be designed into rainwater gardens, retention strips, retention flower beds, and ecological tree pools.

Bioretention facilities present in a variety of forms, and can be widely applied and easily integrated into landscape. However, in areas with a high level of underground water and lithosphere, poor permeable soil and comparatively steep terrain, necessary measures such as soil replacement, seepage-proofing, and construction of steps need to be adopted; therefore, the construction costs will increase.

Rainwater wetlands

Constructing rainwater wetlands is a highly effective measure for controlling pollution of overland runoff. They have high plant coverage, and are usually areas with a small distance between the underground water level and the soil surface, or have sufficient space to form an aquifer. Rainwater wetlands can effectively control discharge of pollutants, reduce flood peak, and adjust and cut down the volume of runoff, thereby relieving erosion of downstream areas. Rainwater wetlands are characterized by high-buffer capacity, low cost, good treatment effects, easy operation and management, low operation and maintenance costs, and low energy consumption. They also create a good ecological environment for large numbers of animals and plants.

Green roof

Green roof, also called planted roof or roof greening, can be categorized into simple green roofs and roof gardens, according to the depth of planting substrates and complexity of landscaping. The depth of substrates is determined by the requirements of plants and roof load. The depth of substrates of simple green roofs is usually less than 6 inches (150 millimeters), while that of garden-type green roofs can surpass 24 inches (600 millimeters). Green roofs can be applied to flat roofs that meet requirements for roof load and waterproofing. They can be also used for pitched roofs with a gradient not more than 15 degrees. Green roofs can effectively reduce gross volume of roof runoff and runoff pollutants. They can conserve energy and cut down emissions, but the strict requirements for roof load, waterproofing, gradient, and space must be met.

Novo Nordisk Nature Park

The park's overall design concept is founded on great thinkers such as Søren Kierkegaard and Friedrich Nietzsche, who came up with their best ideas while walking. Modern research has shown that people become more informal, more relaxed, and more creative and open to new ideas when they are outside. This is especially true when they walk in nature that is wild, untamed, natural, and varied in its expression.

Thus, in Novo Nordisk Nature Park, this knowledge has been used to create a lush nature park with a range of dense biotopes intersected by winding paths, dividing up the many different types of nature in the park. The park thus accentuates the aesthetic experience of nature, and is tailored to provide the greatest sensuous variation of light, shadow, smells, colors, and sounds.

The paths wind up and down through the park's topography, and in and out of biotopes to create maximum spatial variety. The paths provide general access around the site and from one building to another, but they also make it convenient for employees to meet their colleagues and arrange walk-and-talk meetings outdoors. The paths never lead the shortest way between two points, but wind between the biotopes in order to make each trip long enough for the employees to think creatively and meet others on their way. Wild nature, crooked trees, chance meetings with colleagues, birdsong, and rosy cheeks have all become a natural part of a standard working day at Novo Nordisk.

The nature park itself uses a wide palette of native plants, and holds more than 1000 new trees, which will grow into clearly defined small 'forests' and self-regulatory biotopes. The vegetation is designed to be wild and self-sustaining, which allows the biotopes to evolve with natural succession and minimal care. Because of the designer's stated desire to create maximum biodiversity in the park, several dead trees have been placed in between the newly planted trees. Dead tree trunks are vital for natural ecosystems, as they are important habitats for beetles, caterpillars, and mosses. They also provide the park with the smell of decay, the rot of the trunks, and a direct confrontation with the life and death of nature's ecosystem. It is a powerful exhibition of the full aesthetic feeling of nature.

The nature park's 1000 trees were all inspected and hand-picked by the designers in specially selected nurseries, and arranged in relation to their natural habitat, their shape, their volume, and the local microclimate to maximize shelter for the users of the park and for the office buildings. The trees also help to absorb rainwater that falls on the site. Depressions are planted with alder trees and other water-tolerant species in order to contribute to the park's ambitious climate adaptation design. As such, Novo Nordisk Nature Park is the first park in Scandinavia with a 100 percent natural water balance: all rainwater that falls in the area and on the buildings is collected and used for irrigation. Because of the landscape's carefully designed topography and plantation, the nature park can even handle rare torrential rainfall events without directing any water into the sewers.

Location |
Bagsværd, Denmark
Completion date |
2014
Site area |
7.7 acres (3.1 hectares)
Landscape design |
SLA
Collaborators |
Henning Larsen Architects (building architect), Orbicon (climate adaption engineer), Alectia (engineer),

SkælskørAnlægsgartnere (landscape contractor), Urban Green (biotopes)
Client |
Novo Nordisk
Photography |
Torben Petersen & SLA Architects
Awards |
1st place, ForeningenHovedstadensForskønnelse's Architecture Award 2014, Scandinavian Green Roof Award 2014 ; Nominated for The In-Situ Prize by Dansk Beton

Lighting also plays an integral part in the design of the nature park. During the daytime, the sunlight allows the vegetation and the leaves to cast weaving shadows on the gleaming white concrete paths. In the evening, the landscape is lit by carefully aligned tones of white light, which highlight and enhance the natural colors and movements of the vegetation. Some biotopes are enlightened from within by varying Gobo light projections that create the atmosphere of shifting moonlight.

All in all, Novo Nordisk Nature Park provides Novo Nordisk with a strong, new landscape brand, while employees, clients, the citizens of Bagsværd, and the local wildlife all have a sensuous and lush landscape that provides room for recreation, inspiration, and social meetings, and a stress-free environment all year round.

Site plan

1 | 2 | 3
4

1. With more than 2000 newly planted trees and lush vegetation, the park creates new biotopes and improves the microclimate around the two new buildings
2. The flowing path system encourages walk-and-talk brainstorms and chance meetings between co-workers, and creates a healthy work environment with enhanced opportunities for knowledge-sharing and innovation
3. With functional green roofs, the nature park also rises above and into the buildings themselves
4. Novo Nordisk Nature Park is designed to be open to the public and is a large, green and welcoming gesture to the local community. Thus the park fully complies with Novo Nordisk's ambitious triple bottom line principle of environmental, social, and economic sustainability

1│2

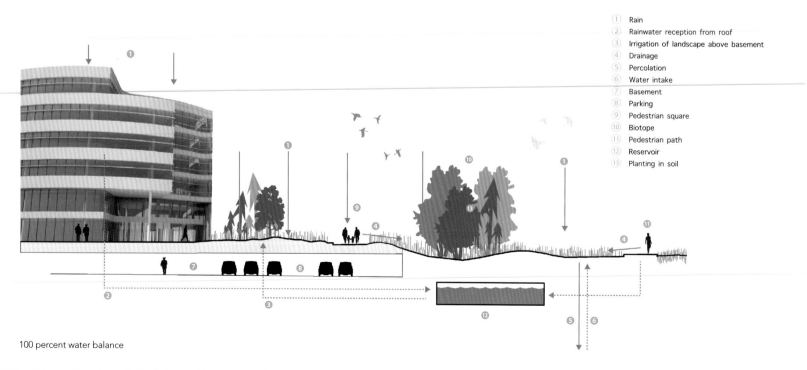

1. Rain
2. Rainwater reception from roof
3. Irrigation of landscape above basement
4. Drainage
5. Percolation
6. Water intake
7. Basement
8. Parking
9. Pedestrian square
10. Biotope
11. Pedestrian path
12. Reservoir
13. Planting in soil

100 percent water balance

1. Novo Nordisk Nature Park is the first landscape in Denmark with 100 percent water balance. This means that all rainwater is being naturally percolated or reused for irrigation in the park or in the building
2. The park has an extensive lighting design which makes the park open and accessible to the public even in the evening and during the long Scandinavian winters

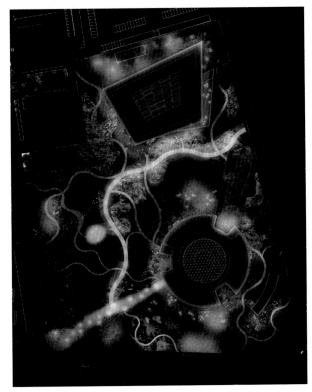

The lighting master plan

Lexington Environmental Education Wetland Classroom

The Lexington Environmental Classroom is an environmentally responsible and engaging outdoor teaching site designed to reconnect students to their environment. Students experience firsthand the importance and impact of environmentally responsible principles through a series of playful rainwater harvesting elements and a wetland / bioretention garden.

Previously, runoff from the building was directed into the area through a system of gutters and downspouts. This runoff then flowed across a poorly maintained lawn that was heavily sprayed with herbicides and pesticides. Catch basins and subsurface drainage captured the contaminated water and deposited it into a nearby bayou.

The first step to transforming the space was the removal of the turf, thus eliminating any future chemical applications and contamination. This high-maintenance turf was replaced with decomposed granite to create a usable surface that would still allow for infiltration. An existing 4-foot (1.2-meter) walk that framed the spaced was retained. The areas between the walk and the building became spaces for each classroom to take ownership of and practice organic gardening.

The next step was to address the poor management of runoff from the site. Thirteen downspouts were removed and replaced with scuppers created from repurposed I-beams from a local scrap yard. These structures capture the water and carry it overhead, bridging the existing walk. The water is then deposited into cisterns that have been fitted with hand pumps. Students are now able to collect the harvested water to nurture their gardens. Excess runoff from the cisterns is directed into river rock–lined troughs that lead to a wetland garden. This sunken garden has the capacity to hold and naturally filter the excess runoff while keeping it on-site. Native wetland plantings including rush, iris, palmetto, and cypress, and other plants are featured in the bioretention garden.

The design elements were arranged to provide flexible and multi-use areas. Seating in these areas are simple log sections repurposed by the student body from a fallen tree on campus. These areas are transformed into classrooms for science experiments, outdoor reading rooms, and a backdrop for art classes.

The outdoor classroom structure is situated in the middle of the bioretention garden. This structure and its location immerse students and visitors in an outdoor setting, allowing them to experience firsthand the natural processes around them.

Just like the runoff and subsurface drainage, 'Out of sight, out of mind' was the theme. However, since project completion, all classroom windows are now open to the garden. Every rain event excites the student body and becomes a teaching opportunity!

Location |
Monroe, Louisiana, United States
Completion date |
2011
Site area |
14,423.6 square feet (1340 square meters)
Landscape design |
Tony Tradewell, ASLA Landscape Architect
Client |
Lexington Elementary Parent Teacher
Organization
Awards |
2012 LA-ASLA Presidents Award of Excellence

1. Covered walkway
2. Art room
3. Existing walkway
4. Outdoor classroom stump seating
5. Education pavilion
6. Classrooms
7. Outdoor classroom
8. Reading room

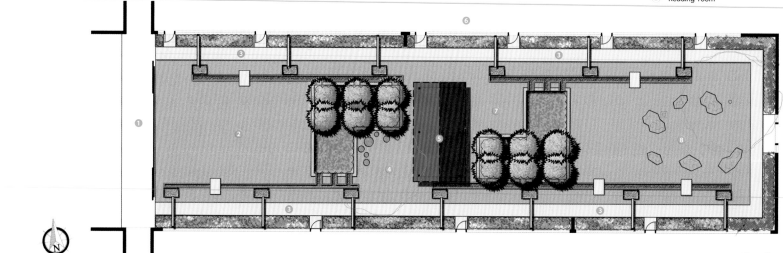

Site plan

1. Seating was created from a fallen tree on-site. Students enjoy rearranging the 'seats' to accommodate different activities
2. Narrow rock-lined troughs carry runoff and overflow from cisterns to the sunken wetland garden at the center of the classroom
3. Existing conditions. Note all water was piped to nearest water body. 'Out of sight, out of mind' was the approach to site drainage

1. Decomposed granite
2. Sunken rain garden, wetland plants filtration recharge zone; overflow goes to existing subsurface drainage
3. Outdoor classroom area, tree-stump seating
4. Classroom pavilion
5. Path around building
6. Sunken rain garden, wetland plants filtration recharge zone; overflow goes to existing subsurface drainage
7. Decomposed granite

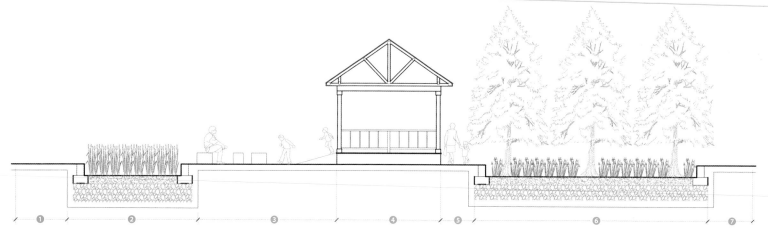

Section plan

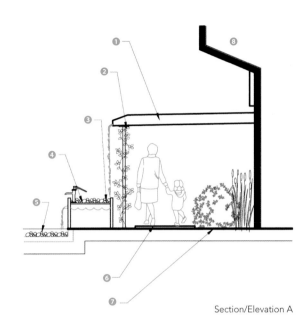

Section/Elevation A

1. The perimeter of the garden is broken up into 10 organic gardens. Each adjacent class is responsible for the care of their garden
2. Students collect water from the cisterns using hand pumps and can utilize the collected water to maintain their classroom gardens along the perimeter of the space
3–4. Landscape architects' initial renderings were used to convince the school officials and student body of what was possible

Athens City Center

Changing the heart of Athens into a true contemporary metropolitan city center requires transformation of the city triangle into a lively and attractive part of the city. The designers put innovative theories of climate control, reduction of vehicular movement, and programming public realm into practise, and then went one step beyond.

The new generation of projects includes green and water systems, which link many ongoing initiatives. The proposal includes a heat-mitigation strategy that will result in a temperature reduction of 2.7–5.4 degrees Fahrenheit (1.5–3 degrees Celsius) during a hot summer day, and the area will be self-sufficient for water, based on the construction of Europe's largest water-retention system, a scale that has never been realized before.

The project focuses on three pillars, creating a resilient, accessible, and vibrant place.

The city center of Athens will be transformed into a green network, and there will be a central green spine, providing shade and shelter. The resilient strategy includes specific attitudes towards reducing the urban heat and improving thermal comfort (natural cooling by greening and shading public spaces, green roofs and façades, cool pavement), reducing air pollution, decreasing energy use, and resolving water issues (stormwater retention and irrigation). Turning the city triangle into a green framework, transforming its corners into green areas, and connecting this framework to the green hills around the city center, result in mitigation of urban heat in the metropolitan center. A greening strategy for Athens is combined with a water strategy, since a good condition of plantings is crucial for heat reduction. Capturing rainwater in underground basins, on top of roofs, or elsewhere helps to keep the water in the area. Besides the technical solutions, water will be used in a poetical way with the underground Eridanosriver.

The green framework will be treated as a coherent network of public spaces in all directions, linking the adjacent neighbourhoods. Restoration of the continuities of the boulevards, the crossing streets, and the squares, creates continuity in the walking experience. By making the new tramline clear and present and part of the grandeur of the space, it contributes to the required cohesion. In fact, the area around Syntagma, Panepistimiou, Omonia, and Patission provides shared space, a new balance between slow traffic and motorized movement. These will be places to be instead of no-go areas: Omonia Square will become Dikaiosynis Square, a green urban square with prominent lush water elements. In the middle of Panepistimou Street, a green ensemble ties the university together into an urban park.

Location |
Athens, Greece
Completion date |
2017–2018
Site area |
56 hectares (138.4 acres)
Landscape design |
OKRA
Collaboration |
MixstUrbanisme, NAMA, LDK,

Roland Jeol, Studio75,
WageningenUniversiteit,
Werner Sobek Green
technologies
Client |
Onassis Foundation
Photography |
OKRA

new city centre 56 ha

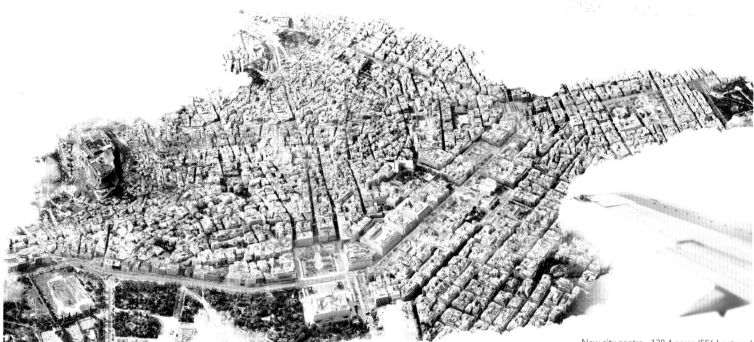

New city centre , 138.4 acres (556 hectares)

Resilent city with a green network

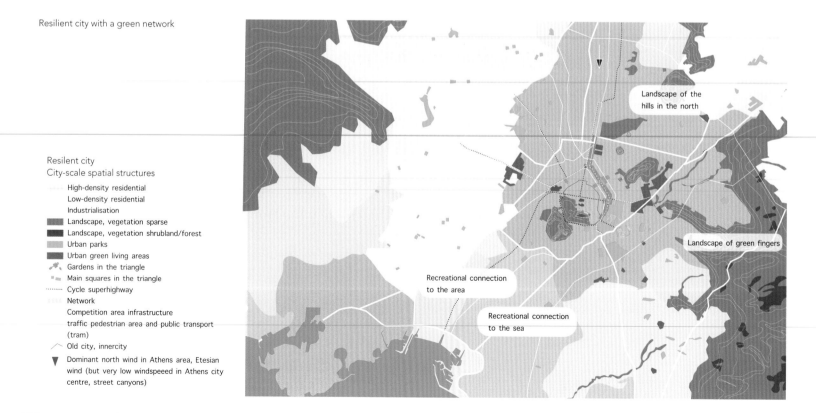

Resilent city
City-scale spatial structures

High-density residential
Low-density residential
Industrialisation
Landscape, vegetation sparse
Landscape, vegetation shrubland/forest
Urban parks
Urban green living areas
Gardens in the triangle
Main squares in the triangle
Cycle superhighway
Network
Competition area infrastructure
traffic pedestrian area and public transport
(tram)
Old city, innercity
Dominant north wind in Athens area, Etesian
wind (but very low windspeeed in Athens city
centre, street canyons)

Landscape of the
hills in the north

Landscape of green fingers

Recreational connection
to the area

Recreational connection
to the sea

1–2. Newly gained space, as a result of the major step towards a walkable city by reducing car traffic in this area, will be transformed into a vibrant, green, and accessible heart of the city. A green framework will form the connection between boulevards and green spaces

A green network is formed by making green boulevards and green squares

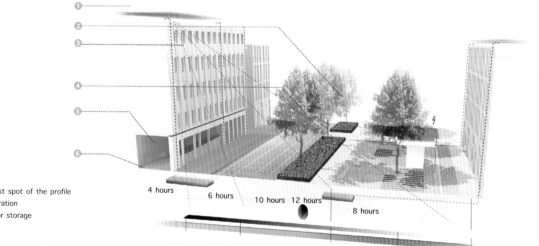

1. Rooftop water collection
2. Solar panels on kiosk roofs
3. Shadow in profile
   Creating shadow through row of trees on the hottest spot of the profile
4. Permeable paving green joints to ensure water infiltration
5. Rainwater collecting/infiltration stormwater crates for storage
6. Hours of exposure to sun in the existing profile

In addition to drought, heat stress calls for action. A strategy of greening, combined with a water strategy allows for a substantial reduction of the urban heat and a pleasant microclimate

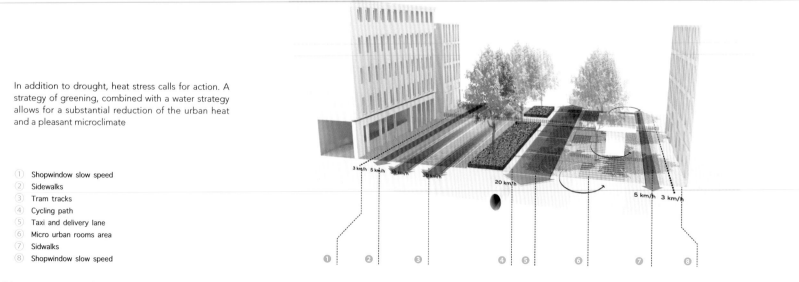

1. Shopwindow slow speed
2. Sidewalks
3. Tram tracks
4. Cycling path
5. Taxi and delivery lane
6. Micro urban rooms area
7. Sidwalks
8. Shopwindow slow speed

Average air temperature, 93.2°F (34°C) in August

before

Hot air

Average temperature reduction: 3°C
Surface temperature reduction: -29%
Thermal comfort index (PET) reduction: -28%

after

To increase the quality of green for the immediate living and working areas, a great diversity of places is created by defining for each green space a characteristic atmosphere. The urban climate will be improved; temperatures during a hot summer day will decrease

1. The formerly unsafe and inhospitable places are transformed into recreational places
2. Dikaiosynis Square

1. Omonia and Dikaiosynis will be green squares with water features. In the middle of the Odós Panepistimiou will be a green strip. The squares are connected to each other
2. The rich patterned panels as both horizontal and vertical elements of the elegant pool canopy
3. The streets perpendicular to Panepistimiou and Patision will be part of the activated network of public spaces
4. People walking into one shop

```
1 | 3 | 4
  2 |
```

In Athens traffic will be rebalanced, changing from vehicular movement to public transport, cycling and walking resulting in pedestrian friendly spaces and larger sidewalks

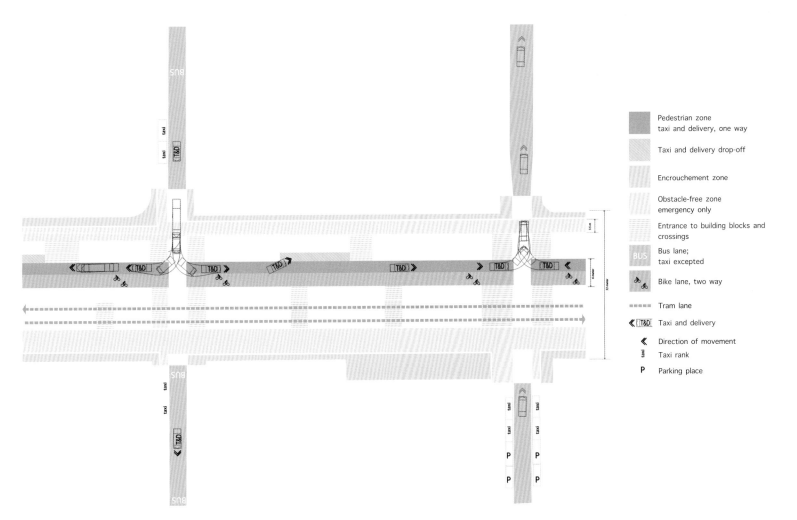

Pedestrian zone
taxi and delivery, one way

Taxi and delivery drop-off

Encrouchement zone

Obstacle-free zone
emergency only

Entrance to building blocks and crossings

BUS Bus lane;
taxi excepted

Bike lane, two way

Tram lane

T&D Taxi and delivery

Direction of movement

taxi Taxi rank

P Parking place

1. The blocks will be used in semi-public places
2. Turf railway in front of one building

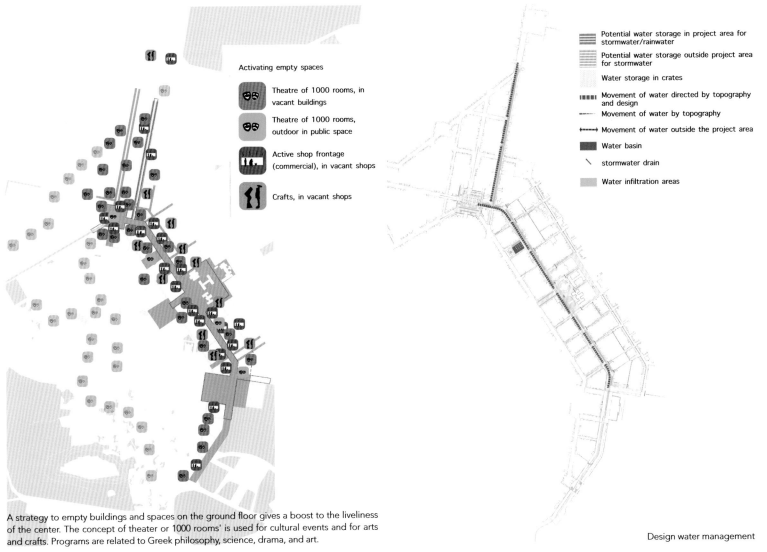

Activating empty spaces

Theatre of 1000 rooms, in vacant buildings

Theatre of 1000 rooms, outdoor in public space

Active shop frontage (commercial), in vacant shops

Crafts, in vacant shops

Potential water storage in project area for stormwater/rainwater

Potential water storage outside project area for stormwater

Water storage in crates

Movement of water directed by topography and design

Movement of water by topography

Movement of water outside the project area

Water basin

stormwater drain

Water infiltration areas

A strategy to empty buildings and spaces on the ground floor gives a boost to the liveliness of the center. The concept of theater or 1000 rooms' is used for cultural events and for arts and crafts. Programs are related to Greek philosophy, science, drama, and art.

Design water management

Confluence Banquets and Resort

Located in the outskirts of Chennai at Mahabalipuram, Confluence is a unique project in its scale and aspiration.

The landscape around the building presents itself in the form of large planters integrated with the ceremonial steps, bringing a human scale and softening the edges. Within the convention building there is a small courtyard designed to allow light and greenery inside the building. Overlooked by the long main corridor and the banquet room, it is designed as a minimalistic garden. A group of plumeria plants forms the key focal point of the courtyard, while layers of shrub plantings sit along the edges of the garden.

Along the side of the convention building runs a linear park all the way to the other end of the site, connecting all three zones. This linear park acts both as a green buffer along the development, and as a garden integrating a linear swale as part of sustainable drainage strategy.

Zone B focuses on the grand lawn separating the convention area and the villa resort area. The lawn, with its vast green carpet, forms an ideal spot for outdoor events. It also forms the perfect foreground for the impressive convention building.

Beyond the central lawn lies zone C, the villa zone, the key landscape zone of the master plan. It is this zone that gives the development its intimate resort feel and character. Overlooking a lush central garden with a series of pavilions and platforms, it acts both as a refuge as well as a green setting for the villas and chalets. An extended rectangular landscape pavilion set at the edge of the pool frames the central garden and acts as a viewing gallery. The carved, sculpted pattern creates a unique set of shadows, adding a dramatic layer of texture on the wall and the floor. In no other area of the project is the lighting as important as it is here. Subtle lighting highlights key features within the landscape, and creates a sublime atmosphere for guests to enjoy.

The Mahabalipuram area has a strong history of granite sculpture dating back thousands of years. In this project, local artists played a critical role in creating the sculptural forms of the monolithic seats in the landscape, as well as the rich textures on the walls and pavilions. The landscape design in this project displays the fact that local art and culture can be woven intricately into a design that is simple yet contemporary.

Location |
Chennai, India
Completion date |
May 2014
Site area |
9.88 acres (4 hectares)
Landscape design |
One Landscape Design Ltd
Client |
Arun Excello
Photography |
MiA Studio

1. The intimate setting of the pool villa garden
2. The panoramic vista of the central swimming pool
3. The intricate pattern of the pool pavilion wall against rich landscape setting

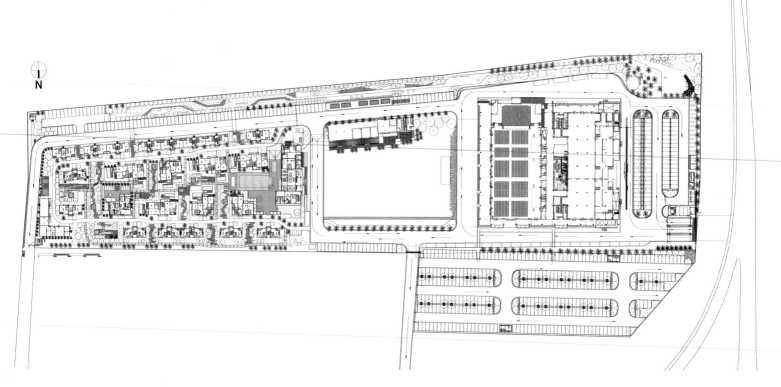

Site plan

1. The central garden with its rich interplay of landscape elements
2. The framing of the evening sun
3. The pavilion as a glowing sculpture set in the garden
4. The elegant poolside pavilion as destination dining

```
 1 | 4
 2 | 3
```

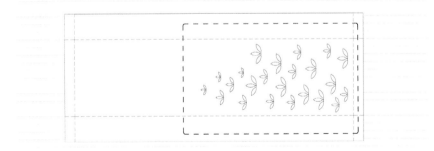

Poolside pavilion plan

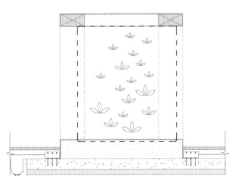

Poolside pavilion section 1

Poolside pavilion section 2

1. The linearity of the garden walls against the textured softscape
2. The play of shadow on the sculptural garden walls
3. The central garden set against a dramatic sky

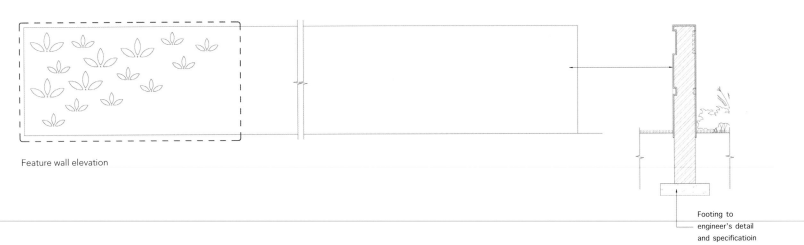

Feature wall elevation

Footing to
engineer's detail
and specificatioin

Feature wall section

Feature wall reference image

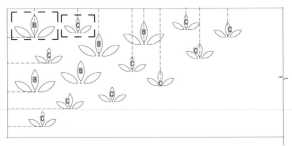

Pattern detail

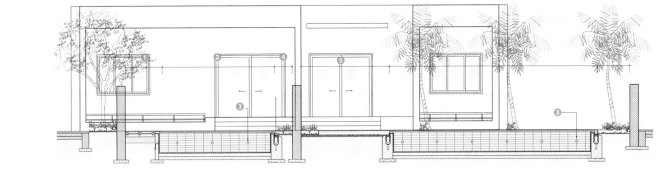

1. Timber deck
2. Plunge pool
3. Pool light
4. Planting area
5. Gravel
6. Timber fixing as per engineer's details
7. Steel grate

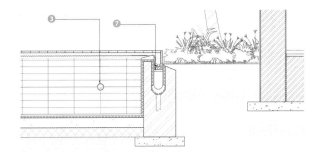

Plan detail of lanscape outside of honeymoon suite

Sheffield Reservoir

The Sheffield Reservoir project converted a 40-million-gallon, open-air reservoir into an open park with an underground water-storage facility. More stringent federal drinking-water regulations led to the renovation of the site, which was no longer meeting the requirements for safe drinking water as an uncovered reservoir.

The design process brought together several city committees and neighbors from the affluent community, along with designers from Van Atta Associates to identify design criteria. Project goals included the construction of two buried concrete reservoirs, creation of a public open space with facilities to support emergency personnel, integration of an existing fire-resistant demonstration garden, and preservation of on-site historic elements to celebrate the area's rich water history.

The resulting 20-acre (8-hectare) park in the foothills of Santa Barbara, California, consists entirely of native plantings propagated from a nearby city nature park to preserve the local species. Regional plant communities, including riparian and oak woodlands, oak savannah, and chaparral, were established on the site in response to new topography and microclimates. Bioswales planted with wetland species create habitats, and treat runoff before it enters Sycamore Creek. A pollinator park was developed to revive the bee colonies in the area. Meaningful elements of the original reservoir, dam, and native-stone drainage channels were preserved and made a part of the trail system, resulting in visual hints of the history of the site. The community now enjoys the benefits of a park with rolling topography, expansive views of the local mountains, and an extensive network of pathways and trails for exploration and recreation.

Site plan

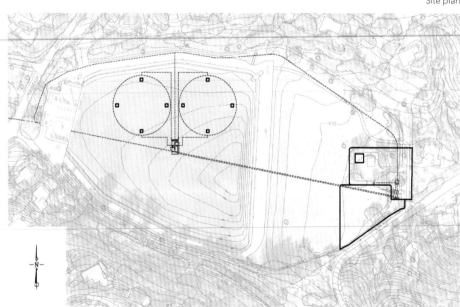

Location |
Santa Barbara, California, United States
Site area |
20 acres (8 hectares)
Landscape design |
Van Atta Associates, Inc.
Client |
City of Santa Barbara
Photography |
Lucia Ferreira

1. Although no longer functioning, the historic 1925 Sheffield Filtration Building remains
2. Original boulders indicate the walls of the historic reservoir

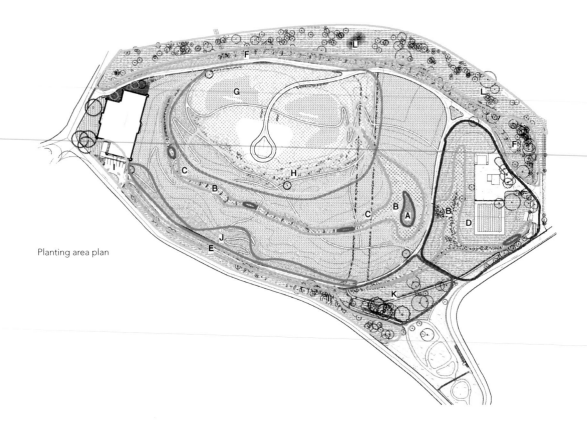

Planting area plan

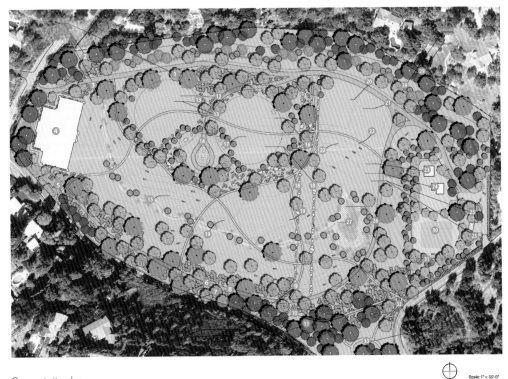

Concept site plan

Scale: 1" = 50'-0"

1. Oak woodland
2. Split-rail fence north of riparian area
3. Historic parapet wall
4. Existing filtration building
5. Sheffield open-space parking area
6. Historic parapet wall walk
7. Oak woodland along open-space perimeter
8. Security/service road with planted reinforced sub-base
9. Pedestrian pathway
10. Historic channel walk
11. Existing eucalyptus/oak woodland
12. Reservoir service road
13. Proposed reservoirs
14. Proposed reservoir vault and ventilation service area
15. Bioswale with check dams
16. Rock outcropping with mosaic pattern chaparral planting
17. Security fencing with informal native screen planting
18. Stacked boulders (limits of old Sheffield reservoir dam)
19. Wildflower and native-grass meadow in oak savanna
20. 8 feet (2.4 meters) clear vegetated passing lane
21. 14 feet (4.3 meters) clear service/fire drive
22. Fire staging open space
23. Proposed control building
24. Existing pump station
25. Concrete channel to remain
26. Summer crossing
27. Retention pond with native planting
28. Natural creek drainage channel with riparian planting
29. Property line and existing fence
30. K-9 training facility
31. Security fencing with informal native screen planting
32. Split-rail fence along open-space perimeter
33. Existing fire demonstration garden

Dry stack boulder wall section and photograph
Scale: 0.75 inches = 1 foot

Boulder retaining wall section
Scale: 1 inch = 10 feet

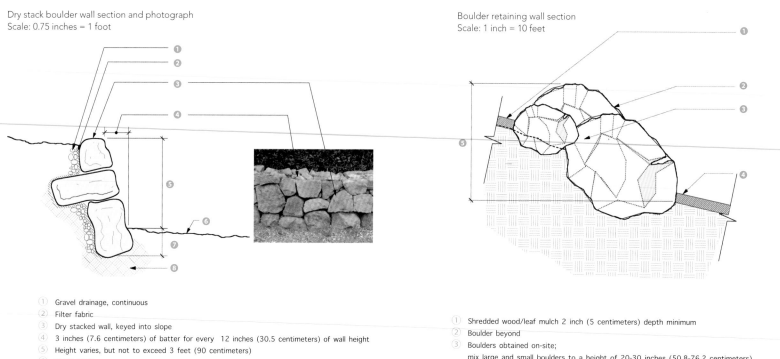

(1) Gravel drainage, continuous
(2) Filter fabric
(3) Dry stacked wall, keyed into slope
(4) 3 inches (7.6 centimeters) of batter for every 12 inches (30.5 centimeters) of wall height
(5) Height varies, but not to exceed 3 feet (90 centimeters)
(6) Finish grade
(7) 12 inches (30.5 centimeters)
(8) 95 percent compacted subgrade

(1) Shredded wood/leaf mulch 2 inch (5 centimeters) depth minimum
(2) Boulder beyond
(3) Boulders obtained on-site;
    mix large and small boulders to a height of 20-30 inches (50.8-76.2 centimeters)
(4) Shredded wood/leaf mulch 2 inch (5 centimeters) depth minimum
(5) 20-30 inches (50.8-76.2 centimeters)

1. The development of a pollinator habitat brought additional bee colonies to the site
2. The creek through the park maintains a summer crossing when the water level runs low
3.The area draws joggers and dog-walkers to enjoy the open space

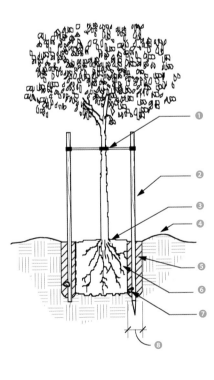

① Locate rubber ties at two-thirds the height of trunk
② Two inch (5.1 centimeter) diameter treated lodge-pole stakes drive into undisturbed subgrade outside root ball
③ Locate crown 1 inch (2.5 centimeters) above existing grade
④ Temporary 4-inch (10.2-centimeter) berm
⑤ Backfill
⑥ Lightly scarify root ball; set on firm pit bottom
⑦ Fertilizer tabs (see specs)
⑧ Six inch (15.2 centimeter) minimum

Notes:
1. Do not damage main roots or destroy root ball when installing tree stakes.
2. To water, backfill 50 percent, irrigate, then complete backfill

Tree planting and staking section
Scale: NTS

Sunshine Cove

Sunshine Cove, adjacent to the Maroochydore CBD, comprises 11 planned precincts of residential, commercial, retail, and community spaces built around a constructed lake. Place Design Group was appointed project landscape architects in 2007, and has provided ongoing design and project management services for the numerous parklands and streetscapes through the development.

The 86 acres (35 hectares) of lake and public open space includes significant linear lakeside parklands. These support a network of recreational and cycling paths, boardwalks, and bridges linking to the nearby retail precinct of Sunshine Plaza and onwards to Cotton Tree beach and the ocean. This urban form challenges streetscape design, providing trees and landscapes to soften the closely located driveways and on-street parking provisions. Compensation for reduced housing setbacks and minimal private open space has been provided through increased landscaping in the streetscape and the creation of small pocket parks, which provide outdoor space for the residents. Streetscape-planting strategies and tree-protection measures were developed to minimize the effects of very limited space for construction activities by home builders.

With all stormwater from the site flowing into the lake system and ultimately out to sea, the local council placed strict conditions on the water quality released from the site. Tate Professional Engineers designed a stormwater treatment system that includes large vegetated swales and bioretention basins in park areas, and smaller narrow bio-retention pods within the street reserve. Innovative planting design was required to ensure that these water-treatment devices were well integrated into the streetscape and landscape character of open park areas. Careful selection of macrophyte species, suitable for planting in the sandy filter media, was required to ensure that plants continued to thrive and look appealing during the drier months.

This high-quality living environment in the dense, urban heart of Maroochydore brings a new form of residential development to the Sunshine Coast, and a strong vision for this new community.

| 1

Location |
Maroochydore, Queensland, Australia
Completion date |
Ongoing
Site area |
86 acres (35 hectares)
Landscape design |
Place Design Group
Client |
Chardan Development Group
Photography |
Elliot Swanson, Carl Spencer

1. Public recreation parkland on the lake edge
2. Lakeside boardwalk and residence
3. Lookout pavilion and walking trail

1 | 2 | 3

Artist impression of above parkland edge

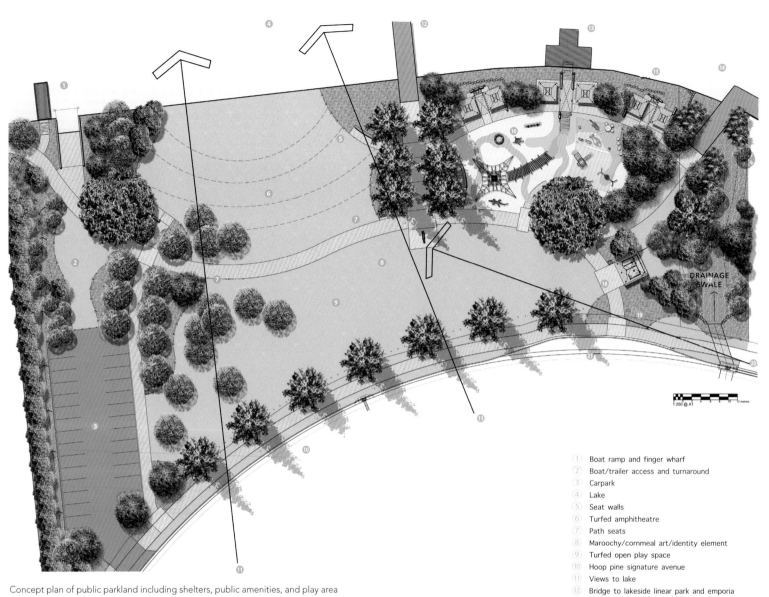

Concept plan of public parkland including shelters, public amenities, and play area

1. Boat ramp and finger wharf
2. Boat/trailer access and turnaround
3. Carpark
4. Lake
5. Seat walls
6. Turfed amphitheatre
7. Path seats
8. Maroochy/cornmeal art/identity element
9. Turfed open play space
10. Hoop pine signature avenue
11. Views to lake
12. Bridge to lakeside linear park and emporia
13. Lake pavilion and wharf
14. Boardwalk
15. Picnic shelters
16. Playground
17. Drainage swale
18. WC
19. Park entry sign
20. View from approach road
21. Bus stop

1–3. Water-sensitive urban design landscape treatments

$\frac{\quad|\quad|3}{1|2|}$

① Seats
② Open-space direction sign and map
③ Main path
④ Hoop pine grove
⑤ Road users glimpse of lake over swale and low plants
⑥ Meander path

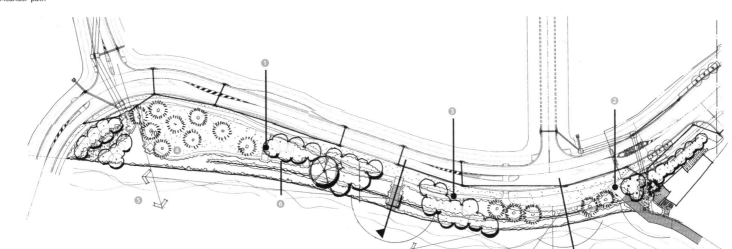

Concept of lakeside area landscape

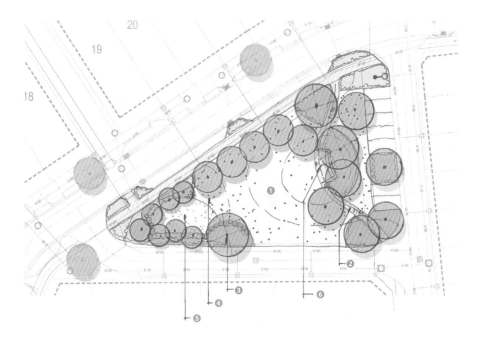

Triangle park-landscap concept plan

1. Turf mound
2. Path
3. Specimen trees typical system
4. Turf flow into water sensitive urban design area
5. Water sensitive urban design area
6. Shade structure/seat wall

1. Ritek roof/shade
2. Bench seating
3. Steel posts/beams
4. Timber bridge/deck
5. Timber kerb
6. Water sensitive urban design area
7. Flagstone column to match existing beam
8. Knek roof/shade
9. Gaw/steel beams
10. Bench seating

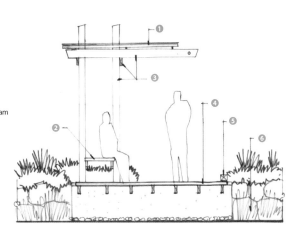

Bridge shade structure concept plan

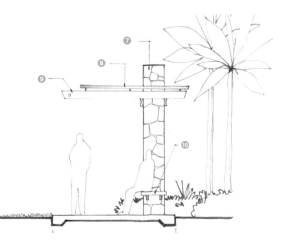

Shade structure with seating concept plan

Avenue park concept plan

1. Entry arbor
2. 1500 wide path
3. Wsud
4. Boulder retain, typical
5. Bbridge seating and shade structure
6. 1800 wide path
7. Entry arbor / shade structure / seating

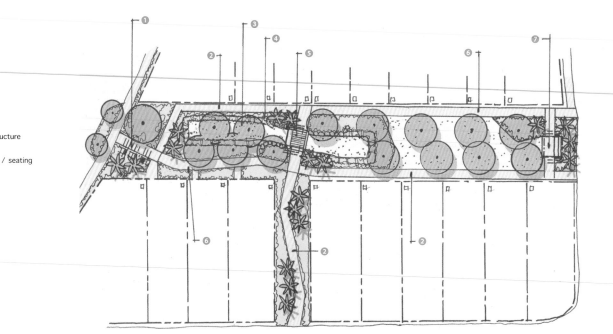

1. View across parkland space
2. Street plantings

Concept plan 1 of northern area landscape

1. Link to future residential area
2. Grassed open space
3. Existing retained grove of trees in this zone
4. Link to existing residential area
5. Boat ramp access with finger wharf
6. Green-turfed play space
7. Lake events viewed from terraces
8. Hoop pine accent grove
9. Pedestrian bridge
10. Central pavilion, roof and pergolas, picnic tables
11. Groundcover and shrubs as safety barrier where path close to lake
12. Boardwalk
13. Mounded screen planting
14. Turfed maintenance access with gate
15. Grassed terraces event space overlooks lake
16. Open turfed play space
17. Twisted deck play element
18. Bollards if conditioned by council
19. Seating wall
20. Hoop pine avenue
21. Overland flow outfall
22. Screen planting
23. Grouted rock retaining wall
24. Avenue of hoop pines opposite park with groundcovers and low shrubs

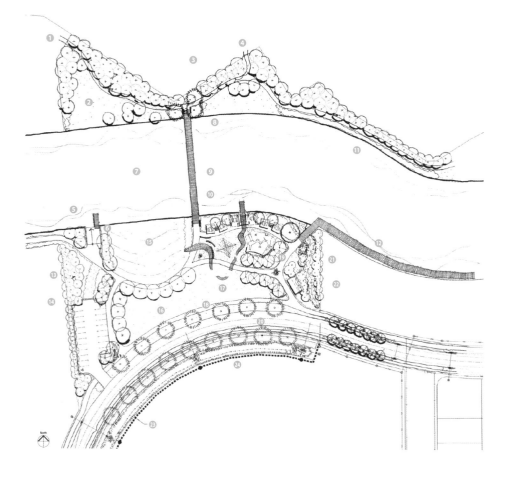

1. Lakeside area at deck
2. One corner of parkland

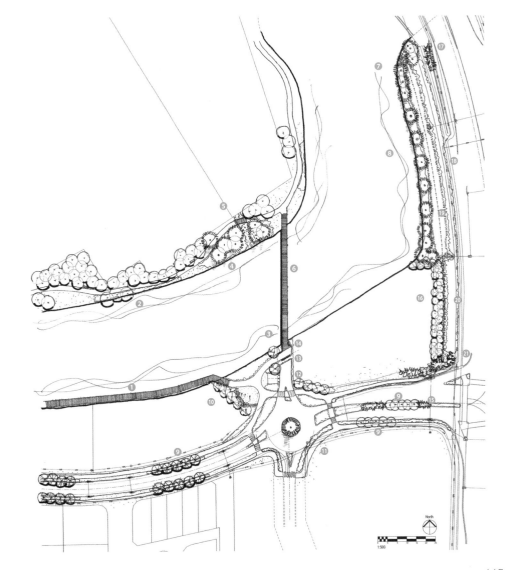

Concept plan 2 of northern area landscape

① Boardwalk
② Groundcover and shrubs as safety barrier where path close to lake
③ Seating on end of bridge
④ Hoop pine accent grove
⑤ Path bridge or culvert over overland flow path from precinct one
⑥ Pedestrian bridge
⑦ Hoop pine accent grove
⑧ Groundcovers under hoop pines along lake edge
⑨ Street trees
⑩ Seating node with views towrds weir and row of markers
⑪ Hoop pine accent in roundabout
⑫ Maintenance vehicle parking
⑬ Low diversion wall
⑭ Potential link to lot
⑮ Palms
⑯ Dense screen planting
⑰ Existing palm grove
⑱ Groundcovers and low shrubs from bloswale to existing footpath
⑲ Reeds and rushes in base of bloswale
⑳ Stones in base of bioswale
㉑ Palm grove to match existing one on boulevard

Saint Mary's Greek Orthodox Church—Campus Renovation and Site Improvements

When designers began talking with Saint Mary's Greek Orthodox Church about their ongoing drainage problems, mobility-access issues, and outdated landscaping back in 2009, designers had yet to realize how comprehensive and sustainable the project that was to develop over the following 2 years was going to be. This project included a wide range of landscape, utilities, accessibility, and stormwater improvements that greatly improved the function, appearance, and sustainability of the church's urban campus located next to a body of water (Lake Calhoun) and adjacent housing, bike trails, and pedestrian paths.

The primary site improvements include new walkways with canopies, planting beds, native trees, memorial monuments, and a wide variety of stormwater best management practices (BMPs). This multifaceted network of stormwater BMPs includes four underground storage chamber systems, permeable pavers, an infiltration basin, a detention basin, and five rain gardens. These stormwater BMP designers carefully designed to effectively manage 96 percent of stormwater runoff produced by the 10-year rainfall event (4.2 inches [10.7 centimeters] in 24 hours) that was previously leaving the site completely untreated. This water now remains entirely on-site via storage, retention, infiltration, and passive reuse for irrigation of the rain gardens. This project also achieved significant water-quality improvements including an 80 percent reduction of total suspended solids (TSS) and more than 65 percent reduction of phosphorus.

As a result of this multi-functional campus renovation, the church successfully achieved 'pre-settlement' stormwater conditions along with eliminating the foundation water-leakage problem, improving the flow of traffic, providing complete accessibility, and greatly enhancing the landscape beds and entryways to the church. This project continues to serve as an excellent example of multi-functional green spaces and resourceful stormwater management.

Location |
Minneapolis, Minnesota, United States

Site area |
3.5 acres (1.4 hectares)

Completion date |
2011

Landscape design |
Solution Blue, Inc.

Client |
Saint Mary's Greek Orthodox Church—
Parish Council

Photography |
Mitchell Cookas of Solution Blue, Inc.

Awards |
Watershed Heroes 'Excellence in
Development' Award from Minnehaha
Creek Watershed District (2011)

Best Congregation Rain Garden Award
from Metro Blooms (2012)

1. Instructing underground chambers
2. New rain gardens and church sign
3. New permeable pavers
4. New rain gardens in front of church

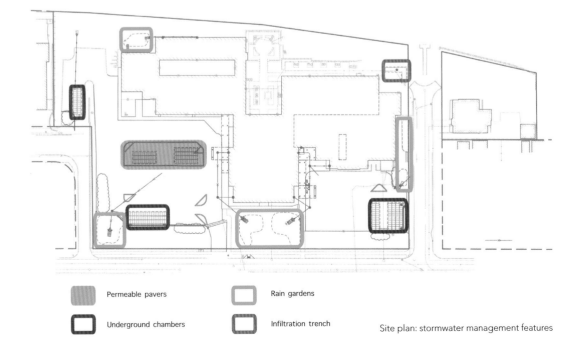

Permeable pavers

Underground chambers

Rain gardens

Infiltration trench

Site plan: stormwater management features

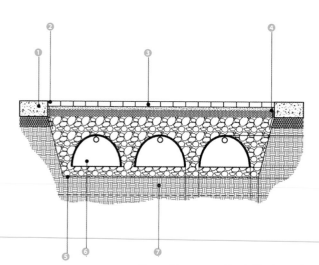

1 | 2 | 5
3 | 4

① 12 x 9 inches (304.8 x 228.6 millimeters) ribbon curb

② Permeable interlocking concrete pavers

③ Joints to be filled with approved materials

④ See detail below for termination bar detail including liner skirt installation

⑤ AASHTO M288 class 2 nonwoven geotextile or approved equal

⑥ Triton stormwater chamber model S-29 or approved equal

⑦ Remove existing soils to 190.0 and replace with washed concrete sand and
   compact to a maximum compaction of 85 percent standard proctor density

Permeable paver parking infiltration tank

Infiltration tank

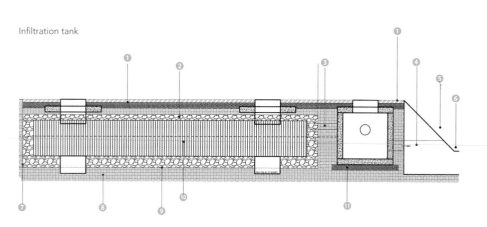

① 4 inches (101.6 millimeters) bituminous
   8 inches (203.2 millimeters) minimum class 5 base aggregate

② 1.5 inches (38.1 millimeters) to 3 inches (76.2 millimeters) diameter
   washed granite or approved equal

③ 6 inches (152.4 millimeters) diameter PVC schedule 80 storm sewer pipe

④ 12 inches (304.8 millimeters) HDPE pipe

⑤ Adjacent bioretention pond 19P-2

⑥ Design detail for energy dissipation

⑦ Vertical slope represent final product, contractor to ensure proper and
   safe trench side wall slopes are constructed and maintained at all times

⑧ Approved subgrade to be flat, rip existing soils 12 inches (304.8 millimeters)
   to maximum compaction of 85 percent standard proctor density

⑨ AASHTO M288 class 2 nonwoven geotextile or approved equal to be
   installed on all sides between washed granite and subgrade

⑩ Triton storm water chamber model S-29 or approved equal

⑪ 6 inches (152.4 millimeters) minimum class 5 base aggregate

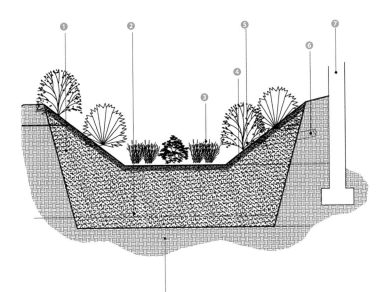

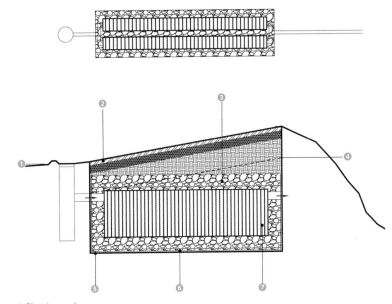

Bio-retention

① Top 24 inches (609.6 millimeters) of profile to be 70/30 (washed concrete sand grade 2 compost) maximum
② Bottom 36 inches (914.4 millimeters) of profile to be washed concrete sand
③ See landscape plan for bioretention plant species
④ 3 inches (76.2 millimeters) shredded hardwood mulch
⑤ Energy dissipation
⑥ 12 inches (304.8 millimeters) diameter pipe from adjacent parking lot
⑦ Existing building
⑧ Approved subgrade, rip existing soils 12 inches (304.8 millimeters) below subgrade to a maximum compaction of 85 percent standard proctor density

Infiltration tank

① 3 x 36 inches (76.2 x 914.4 millimeters) continuous asphalt speed bump to divert water to CBMH-1
② 4 inches (101.6 millimeters) bituminous
   8 inches (203.2 millimeters) minimum class 5 base aggregate to match existing
③ 1.5 inches (38.1 millimeters) to 3 inches (76.2 millimeters) diameter washed, crushed granite type stone or approved equal
④ SP soils at 188.5 feet (57.5 meters) +/- near catch basin end of storage system
⑤ Approved subgrade, rip existing soils 12 inches (304.8 millimeters) below subgrade to a maximum compaction of 85 percent standard proctor density
⑥ AASHTO M288 class 2 nonwoven geotextile or approved equal to be installed on all sides between granite and subgrade
⑦ Triton stormwater chamber model S-29 or approved equal

1. Instructing underground chambers
2. Instructing permeable pavers
3. Instructing pavers in rain garden
4. New permeable pavers and canopy
5. New rain garden and preserved oak tree

Hyde Park Lakes Restoration

A new bioretention system has significantly improved water quality in Hyde Park, Perth's oldest gazetted park, and registered with the Heritage Council of Western Australia as a culturally significant site.

The project transformed the two Hyde Park lakes, addressing issues with silt and acid sulphate soils, water quality, and periodic drying out, and recreated an 'Arcadian landscape' in sympathy with the park's original design.

The bioretention system has been designed to treat minor catchment flows through diversion of stormwater from Hyde Park branch drain into Hyde Park lakes. The project also involved extensive remediation and landscaping works in keeping with the style of park, the heritage significance, and the aesthetics of the local residents and users.

The City of Vincent was very aware of the need for an aesthetically pleasing water system that reflected the status of the park. The system would have to be well integrated into the overall schematics of the park, while treating low-flow storm events to allow for a more constant and cleaner water source for the lakes. It is also expected to substantially reduce the volume of groundwater used to maintain water levels in the lakes.

Instead of a standard sediment tank, the rain-garden system consists of three-tiered bioretention cells controlling the detention and infiltration of the stormwater through a filter media. The system removes the sediment, nitrogen, and phosphorus, as well as retaining the stormwater to mitigate flood events. The filter media is planted with drought-tolerant endemic species, which are able to withstand periodic inundation, and have vigorous root systems to allow for both the uptake of nutrients and to also maintain hydro absorption of the soil. This system treats stormwater from approximately 321 acres (130 hectares) of suburban areas.

With innovative water-quality treatment measures, tasteful aesthetic design and robust construction staging, the project transformed a water system in decline into a thriving, rich, aquatic habitat. The project also shows how rain-garden systems can be retrofitted to enhance the amenity of a culturally significant park, while also enabling flood mitigation in an urban area.

Location |
Perth, Western Australia, Australia
Completion date |
2013
Site area |
2952.8 square feet (900 square
meters)
Landscape design |
GHDWoodhead

Client |
City of Vincent
Photography |
GHDWoodhead
Awards |
Engineers Australia, Western
Australia Division Engineering
Excellence Awards—Environment
and Small Companies categories

(1) Inlet diversion pipe
(2) Inlet pit
(3) Batter with planting slope varies 1:2 to 1:4
(4) Low-flow distribution channel
(5) Existing pathway
(6) Overflow pit
(7) Existing pathway and open space to amphitheater maintained
(8) Proposed timber platform bridge
(9) Rock boulders/swale discharging water to lake
(10) Stone mulch
(11) Filter media (sand)
(12) Transition layer (sand with carbon source)
(13) Gravel drainage layer (with slotted PVC drainage pipe)
(14) HDPE liner

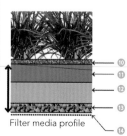

Filter media profile

The layout of the rain garden within the park, which comprises three bioretention cells

1. The bioretention system has been designed to treat minor catchment flows through diversion of stormwater
2. The plants are able to withstand periodic inundation and have vigorous root systems

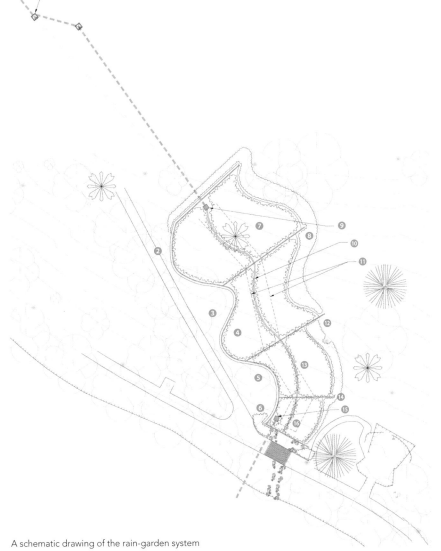

A schematic drawing of the rain-garden system

① Transition pit 47.2 x 47.2 inches (1200 x 1200 millimeters)
② Rain-garden wall tier 1-17.20 TW
③ Rain-garden wall tier 2-16.80 TW
④ Rain-garden tier 2-16.50 RL
⑤ Rain-garden wall tier 3-16.00 TW
⑥ Rain-garden wall tier 4-15.70 TW
⑦ Rain-garden tier 1-16.80 RL
⑧ Rain-garden weir wall tier 1-17.10 TW
⑨ Rain-garden inlet pit 35.4 x 35.4 inches (900 x 900 millimeters)
⑩ 11.8 x 3.9 inches (300 x 100 millimeters) galvanised-steel channel, low-flow distributor
⑪ 11.8 inches (300 millimeters) of slotted pipe
⑫ Rain-garden weir wall tier 2-16.80 TW
⑬ Rain-garden tier 3-15.70 RL
⑭ Rain-garden weir wall tier 3-16.00 TW
⑮ Rain-garden outlet pit 47.2 x 47.2 inches (1200 x 1200 millimeters)
⑯ Rain-garden tier 4-15.40 RL

1. The system removes the sediment, nitrogen, and phosphorus, as well as detaining the stormwater to mitigate flood events
2. Instead of a standard sediment tank, the rain-garden system consists of three-tiered bioretention cells
3. The filter media is planted with drought-tolerant endemic species

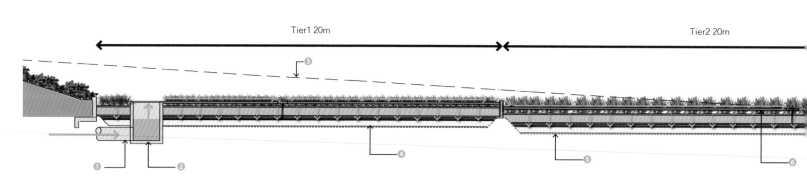

A cross-section of the rain-garden

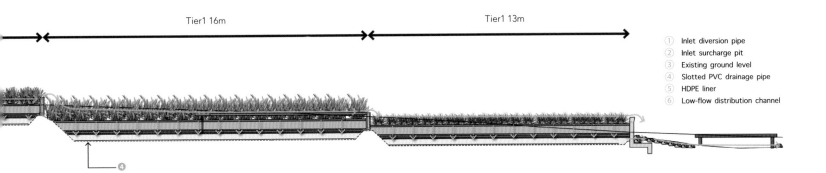

Tier1 16m   Tier1 13m

1. Inlet diversion pipe
2. Inlet surcharge pit
3. Existing ground level
4. Slotted PVC drainage pipe
5. HDPE liner
6. Low-flow distribution channel

6 | Soil Improving and Intelligent Water-saving Technologies

Characteristics of city soil

City soil is the result of human activity over a long time, mainly distributed in parks, roads, stadiums, city watercourses, outskirts, peripheries of enterprises and public institutions, factories, and mines. It may also simply become the 'foundation' of buildings, streets, roads, and other urban and industrial facilities. Compared with natural and agricultural soil, city soil only inherits certain characteristics of original natural soil. Its original microflora has changed along with the natural, physical, and chemical quality of soil being destroyed under influences brought about by human interference. At the same time, some artificial contaminants enter the soil and thus form a kind of special soil that differs from natural and agricultural soil. It has the following characteristics.

The city soil structure is disordered

The layers of city soil are much varied and include non-continuous rock stratum, therefore, the structure, quality, organic contents, pH value, volume weight as well as related air permeability, drainage, water-holding capacity, and fertility status of different layers are remarkably different. Furthermore, some wastes produced in urban production and living, such as buildings and household wastes, broken bricks, bituminous debris, and concrete blocks, need to be treated. Building landfill is one of most frequently used ways to treat wastes. Landfill can blend with soil fragments of natural soil layers. It can change the order of soil layers and the composition of soil. It can also influence the permeability and biochemical characteristics of soil.

The city soil has high compactness and poor permeability

High compactness is a major characteristic of city soil. Due to high density of population and high human traffic, as well as frequent use of all kinds of machinery, the density of soil increases gradually, particularly the areas with frequent human activity such as parks and streets. In these areas, the soil has a very high volume weight and extremely low porosity. The porosity of some heavily compacted subsoil or substrates could be as low as 20–30 percent, sometimes even less than 10 percent. Compaction can damage the soil's structure, increase its volume weight, lower its porosity, and cut its water-holding capacity.

Moreover, high compactness of soil can also influence the movement of solutes and the activities of living creatures, thus it can have a significant impact on the urban environment. For example, the city parks are populated with visitors, and as they tread on the ground, the soil is hardened and permeability decreased. Trees are grown on small tree discs and surrounded by big areas of pavement. Thus the air exchanges between above-ground and underground are affected, and the growing environment of plants deteriorates. As the city soil has heavy volume weight, high hardness and poor permeability, the growth of root systems here is severely inhibited. As the root system is badly developed and even turns dead, the above-ground part

Siree Ruckhachat Nature Learning Park:
Boardwalk along the water's edge providing access to natural habitats

The city soil has high pH value

The city soil has increasingly turned alkaline. Its pH value grows higher than its surrounding natural soil. The soil reaction is mostly ranged from neutral to light alkaline. Light alkaline soil only reduces the effects of iron and phosphorus elements in it, but also impedes the activities of soil micro-organisms and decomposition of other nutrients. For instance, in Taihao mausoleum of Henan province, because the soil contains invaders such as lime and incense ashes, the pH value of the soil around roots of many old cypress trees is around 8.8. Therefore, these cypress trees grow very poorly and are urgently in need of further measures to improve the growing environment; only by this way can these old trees grow healthily. The neighboring areas of some industrial districts may have strong acid reaction in the soil.

The city soil has lots of solid invaders, low content of organic matter, and insufficient mineral elements

As the city soil is mostly construction waste soil, it contains large quantities of bricks and tiles, sand and stones, coal dust, wood refuse, ash residue, and ash pits left by construction of buildings. It often happens that the plants' roots are unable to penetrate the soil and meet restrictions in expanding the depth and span. When the content of solid foreign substance in the oil is good, the soil's air and water permeability can be improved to some extent, so the growth of plants' roots will be promoted. However, when it is in excess, the water-holding capacity of soil will decrease and the organic matter will also fall in short. For example, Zhuo Wenshan and others have carried out research on the soil fertility of greenbelts in seven function districts in Guangzhou city. The results show that, compared with natural soil, city soil is lower in organic and total nitrogen content and high in phosphorous content. The fertility of soil is best in new dwelling districts, worse in parks, and much worse in old industrial districts, new development districts, old dwelling districts, traffic areas, and commercial districts.

City soil organisms have changed

The development of cities gradually eats away the original natural environment and in its place grows artificial landscaping such as bituminous and concrete ground and buildings. The hardening of the city-soil surface, the isolation of habitats of living creatures, the increase of human interference and soil pollution,

of landscaping plants lack water and nutrients. If this situation remains for a long time, the trees will grow increasingly weak and finally wither.

The hardening of city ground obstructs the exchange of water and air between city soil and the surroundings. The permeability of soil is thus brought down, its water stores are greatly decreased, the decomposition of soil organic matter is lowered, and the soil's degradation is aggravated. The environment with poor permeability, nutrition, and water contents badly affects the growth of plants' root systems. The plants may grow weakly, have lower stress resistance, and may even wither.

and other factors have simplified the structure of the edaphic soil community and reduced its diversity. The variety and quality are far less than that of agricultural and natural soil. Furthermore, it is also subject to infection by pathogenic organisms and thus is harmful to humans' health.

For planted landscapes, the soil's water-holding capacity can also decide the consumption of water and electricity of landscaping. Therefore, for landscaping design with lots of planted greenbelts, taking measures to improve the soil and update water-holding capacity are also effective measures for reducing energy consumption.

The water capacity of soil refers to the soil's capacity to absorb and hold water. The absorption and holding of water is finished by capillary attraction of soil pores and molecule attraction of soil particles. These two attractions are called by a joint name of soil attraction, or matrix attraction. Water is an important part of natural soil. It not only influences the soil's physical properties but also restricts the dissolution and transfer of nutrients and activities of micro-organisms.

Factors that affect water-holding capacity of soil

The water-holding capacity of soil can be influenced by many factors, which mainly include structure of soil, overall porosity of soil, capillary porosity, and contents of soil-like organic matter, silt particles, and salinity. As the porosity and silt particles of soil are the major factors, the improvement of the soil's water-holding capacity begins with them.

The structure of soil is the basis for its functions. It is a multilayered unit with pores of different dimensions, formed in the natural process of alternative changes of dry, wet, freezing, and melting conditions, with the participation of soil constitutes such as mineral particles and organisms.

The water-holding capacity of soil is closely related to content and specific surfaces of clay particles. Clay particles are the most active and major components of soil and can greatly affect the soil's water-holding capacity. According to research, the more appropriate the clay particle content of soil and the larger the specific surfaces of clay particles, the greater the soil's electric charge and the more water molecules the soil can attract. Salinity also has a certain influence on the water-holding capacity of soil. Under natural conditions, the soil with higher salinity will have poorer water-holding capacity.

The overall porosity of soil can also affect its water-holding capacity. Soil water is an essential condition for the growth of

plants, while the water conditions are decided by the structure of soil, which is also an important physical property of soil. If the overall porosity of soil is within a reasonable range, its water-holding capacity will be improved. According to studies, the higher the porosity, the poorer the water-holding capacity. Meanwhile, if the porosity is too low, water will also not be able to enter the soil and the water-holding capacity of soil will be reduced.

Improvement of soil's water-holding capacity

Currently, there are three approaches to improve soil's water-holding capacity: non-tillage of soil and straw mulching, mixing of soil, and using water-retaining agents. Non-tillage of soil and straw mulching have excellent effects and are easy to carry out, but they are mainly used for cultivated lands and will be discussed later. The following text will give a simple introduction to mixing of soil and use of water-retaining agents.

Soil mixing

Soil mixing refers to mixing soils with strong and poor water-holding capacities and improving the physical structure of soil so as to achieve water conservation. Scholar Zhuang Jiping has done research on this with dry-density soil, bentonite, and cohesive soil. He designed an orthogonal experiment to study the functions of mixing bentonite with cohesive soil to keep the water-holding and water-conserving capacity of sandy soil. According to the research, the water-holding ratio reduces with the increase of dry-density soil, while it increases with the addition of bentonite and cohesive soil. The optimal combination is with 1.3 grams of dry-density soil per milliliter, 6 percent of bentonite, and 20 percent of cohesive soil. The factors' order is dry-density soil, cohesive soil, and bentonite according to their influences on water-holding capacity of soil in earlier stages, however, the order changes into bentonite, cohesive soil, and dry-density soil in the later stages. In overall consideration of water-holding and water-conserving capacity, the optimal combination is with 1.4 grams of dry-density soil per milliliter, 6 percent of bentonite and 15 percent of cohesive soil. Bentonite and cohesive soil can enhance the water-holding and water-conserving capability of sandy soil.

Using water-retaining agents

Soil water-retaining agents are high-molecular polymers with super water-absorption and water-retention capabilities. They are made of resin that has strong water-absorption capabilities. They can quickly absorb and retain water several hundred, even thousand, times its own weight. Water-retaining agents have high hydrophilia, but cannot dissolve into water, so they can be used repetitively for absorbing water. Water-retaining agents absorb water and swell into hydrogel. The hydrogel can slowly release water for the absorption and use of plants to improve the water-holding capacity and structure of soil as well as the water-use efficiency.

Siree Ruckhachat Nature Learning Park:
Geo-fabric tension is used to stabilize and increase soil-bearing capacity,
soil filling, and soil amendment, helping to add nutrients and provide deeper root zone for plants

Hyllie Plaza

The competition entry for the new plaza in the Hyllie district of Malmö bore the motto *Fagus*, the scientific name for beech. The idea driving the design was to establish a beech forest in the plaza, or the plaza as a beech forest. Being a characteristic species for the region, the beech forest would contribute a regional identity to a site almost without character. The beech tree, then, would be the trademark for the new plaza.

Unfortunately, the design concept was as ignorant as it was unique: beech trees don't thrive in the conditions provided by the site—they would require help. In nature, the growth of the trees depends on free soil with an active exchange of oxygen and carbon dioxide at their roots. Mulch must be perpetually turned over, and the trees benefit from the falling organic debris characteristic of a forest. Beech trees are sensitive to drought. Despite these challenges, the motto for the competition entry was set and the aim of the proposal was no longer negotiable. In response, significant botanical research began, a project that included the efforts of many experts trying to find a high-tech solution for ensuring the life of the Hyllie beech grove.

First, it is a gigantic planting bed that equals the dimensions of the plaza above it. This earthen layer consists of a 31.5-inch-thick (80-centimeter-thick) base of football-sized boulders that form a structure of soil, 60 percent of which is cavities. This volume is filled with watered-down mulch. The planting bed is capped with Swedish high-density granite paving, totalling an area of 3 acres (1.2 hectares). Each paving stone measures 6.6 feet by 3.3 feet (2 meters by 1 meter) and is 4.7 inches (12 centimeters) thick, with sawn sides and a thermal finish. They are laid out with exposed joints in both directions. Into this granite field, 12 parallel slits are cut, each planted with two, three, or four beech trees. The earth in the planting bed in each slit has been mixed with pumice and mycorrhiza. Pumice is petrified lava ash with an outstanding capacity to retain moisture; mycorrhiza is a living mushroom/root mixture that improves the tree's nutrient turnover through symbiosis.

There are 28 beech trees, each 30 years old. They were found in a plant nursery north of Berlin, wrapped on-site, and transported to Malmö with their roots frozen. A blue dot on each trunk recorded the orientation of the tree in the nursery, information vital to its successful replanting in Sweden. A sensor inside the bark of each tree registers the transport of liquids in its cells at every given moment. Hardly the products of the natural forest, these trees are truly 'incubator babies.'

By their placement, the trees form a series of glades on the plaza. Within the glades, seating of various kinds rests on surfaces paved with blocks of wood. Eleven masts, each 52.5 feet (16 meters) tall, are lined up along the sides of the plaza and frame its boundaries. Between the masts stretch 5900 feet (1800 meters) of steel cables, arranged in a certain disorder resembling a spider's web. The cables support a field of 2800 LEDs programmed to four seasonal scenarios that create a digital sky after dark.

Location |
Malmö, Sweden
Completion date |
2011
Site area |
3.5 acres (1.4 hectares)
Landscape design |
Thorbjörn Andersson with Sweco
architects

Design team |
Johan Krikström, Marianne Randers,
PeGeHillinge
Consultant |
Niklas Ödmann (lighting design)
Client |
City of Malmö
Photography |
Kasper Dudzik , Sweco architects, Robert
Kjellen, Åke E:son Lindman, City of Malmoe

1. The concept behind the plaza is to build a stylized beech forest on the plaza. The beech tree is characteristic
   for this southern part of Sweden
2. Four very large water troughs form the entrance zone for the event arena at the northern edge
3. The water circulates by spilling over the tilted sides of the trough. The sides are cladded with Norwegian
   slate mounted like shingles

1
2 3

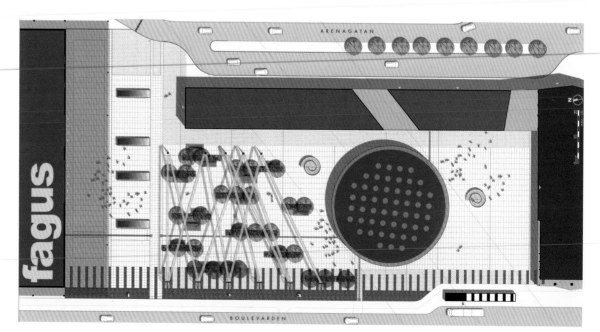

Site plan for Hyllie plaza

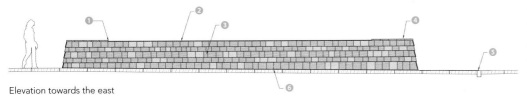

Elevation towards the east

Elevation towards the west

① Waters edge, starting point
② Slate tiles should be roughly cut
③ Slate tiles in two nuances, mounted with overlap
④ Raised edge of water feature
⑤ Linear drainage
⑥ Lowest row of slate tiles should stop 1.2 inches (30 millimeters) above ground

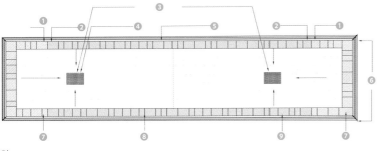

Plan

① Upper edge
② Edge with water overflow
③ Local recess
④ Metal grid that measures 15.7 by 23.6 inches (400 by 600 millimeters)
⑤ Edges to be covered by slate
⑥ See detail at edge of water feature
⑦ Tile of slate, type 8, all visible edges art to be cut
⑧ Waters edge with overflow, tile of slate, visible edges are to be cut
⑨ Overflow edge at level +25,65

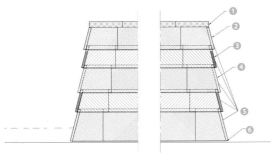

Construction details of the water trough

① Tile of slate, 2 inches (50 millimeters), edges to be cut
② At the corners of the basin, the slate tiles should alternate in the way they meet
③ Edge of slate to be visible
④ Edge of slate to be hidden
⑤ Tiles of slate should be mounted with visible width according to drawing
⑥ Edge of slate should stop 0.4 inches (10 millimeters) above ground

Construction drawing showing the southern end

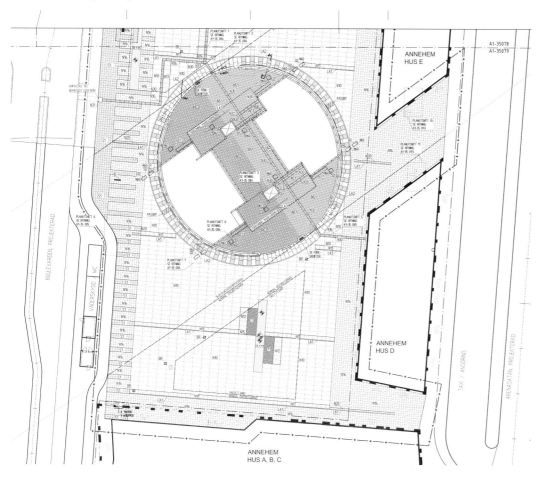

1. The masts have been designed as narrow bookshelves, having spotlights mounted inside of them
2. In the autumn, the beech tree leaves turn golden brown

1. Reinforcement layer
2. Mortar
3. Slate
4. Lamp post
5. *Fagus sylvatica* trees belong to separate contract
6. *Fagus sylvatica* hedge belongs to separate contract
7. Seating
8. Surface of wood put on butt end
9. Geo-textile
10. Reinforcement layer of non-assorted gravel

11. Reinforcement layer of tarmac
12. Adjustment layer
13. Granite
14. Additional reinforcement layer
15. Geo-textile net
16. Return fill
17. Fundament for lamp post
18. Underground pipe for distribution of air and water
19. Tree pit

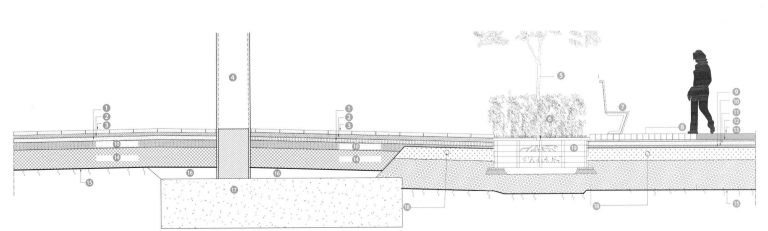

Section showing the tree pits and the structural soil

1–2. The trees are put into slits in the granite floor
3. The park sofas define the social areas, which are the glades

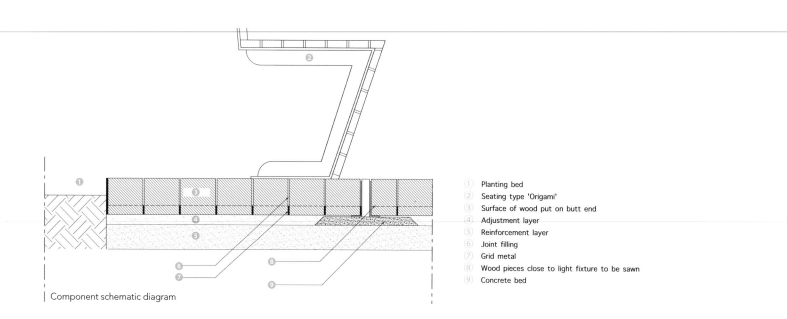

Component schematic diagram

① Planting bed
② Seating type 'Origami'
③ Surface of wood put on butt end
④ Adjustment layer
⑤ Reinforcement layer
⑥ Joint filling
⑦ Grid metal
⑧ Wood pieces close to light fixture to be sawn
⑨ Concrete bed

Section details of seating fundament and soil layers

① Reinforcement layer of non-assorted gravel
② Reinforcement layer of tarmac
③ Adjustment layer
④ Surface of wood put on butt end
⑤ Porous reinforcement layer
⑥ Structural soil
⑦ Terrace with geo-textile net
⑧ Level adjustment
⑨ Tree pit
⑩ Lava pebbles
⑪ Fundament for lamp post
⑫ Lamp post
⑬ Reinforcement layer

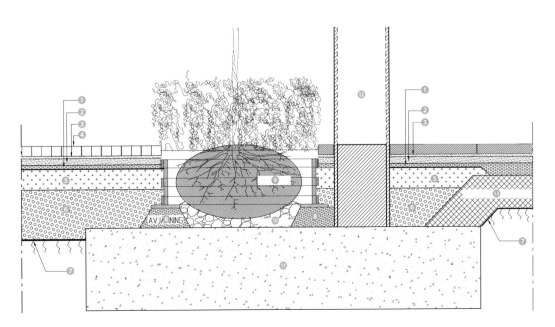

Siree Ruckhachat Nature Learning Park

The Siree Ruckhachati Nature Park is a live laboratory for pharmacy students to make themselves familiar with Thai medicinal plants. The garden, however, also has other objectives, including to serve as a collection and conservation center for Thai medicinal plants; to serve as a cultivation place for medicinal plants needed for research projects; and to be a Thai medicinal plants information center for pharmacy students and traditional Thai medicine students from other universities or institutions, as well as for researchers, health professionals, school students, and others.

The park originally served as the preservation area for a collection of more than 800 species of medicinal plants.

The new park was designed to include three major areas: the Medicinal Plants Active Learning Center, wetland and natural habitat zone, and the Medicinal Plants Genetic Research and Services Center. The design idea is to integrate activities with the existing natural ecology of the site. However, the salty and poor-quality soil, high level of groundwater, and lack of maintenance were major problems and needed urgent improvement.

The redesign and planning of the new park use simple but intelligent techniques to solve the critical problems. Geo-fabric tension sheets are used to stabilize and increase soil-bearing capacity, soil filling, and soil amendment, helping to add nutrients and provide deeper root zones for plants. Water-level management helps to lower the groundwater, and a subdrain was added to help flush the water and dilute the salty soil.

The opening of the park will strengthen and share the knowledge between the campus and the surrounding community. The park also serves as a large green open space for learning and relaxing for local people.

Location |
Nakhonprathom, Thailand
Completion date |
2014
Site area |
137 acres (55.4 hectares)
Landscape design |
Axis Landscape Company Limited

Client |
The Division of Physical and
Environment, Mahidol University
Photography |
Mr. Anawat Pedsuwan, Mr. Ekachai
Yaipimol, Mr. Niphon Fahkrachang,
Miss Theemaporn Wacharatin

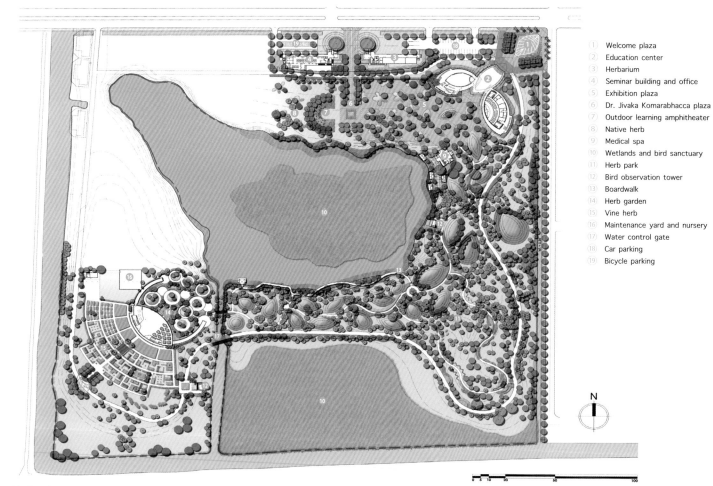

Master plan

(1) Welcome plaza
(2) Education center
(3) Herbarium
(4) Seminar building and office
(5) Exhibition plaza
(6) Dr. Jivaka Komarabhacca plaza
(7) Outdoor learning amphitheater
(8) Native herb
(9) Medical spa
(10) Wetlands and bird sanctuary
(11) Herb park
(12) Bird observation tower
(13) Boardwalk
(14) Herb garden
(15) Vine herb
(16) Maintenance yard and nursery
(17) Water control gate
(18) Car parking
(19) Bicycle parking

(1) Bus stop
(2) Vine herb
(3) Multipurpose lawn
(4) Herb nursery and kitchen
(5) Herb garden
(6) Wetlands and bird sanctuary

Elevation plan 1

(1) Wetlands and bird sanctuary
(2) Exhibition plaza
(3) Education center
(4) Welcome plaza

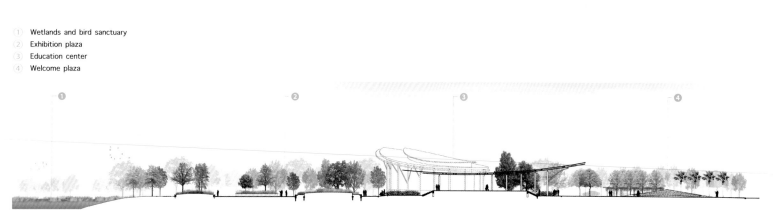

Elevation plan 2

1–2. Plant display in herb park

1. Boardwalk along water edge providing access for users to study water plants and natural habitats
2. Amphitheater, an outdoor classroom located next to medicinal plants exhibit plaza
3. Meandering walkway extends throughout natural plant exhibition zone

1. Floated root due to high level of underground water and salty soil
2. Install water control gate to lower water in internal pond land infill
3. Provide underground drainage system for tree pit and planting area
4. Berm up area for specific type of plant to provide more root zone
5. Provide quality soil and nutrient
6. Protect water edge with wetland plants and enhance ecosystem in the pond
7. Soil dilution through irrigation and drainage proces

Water-level management diagram

① Exhibition plaza
② Dr. Jivaka Komarabhacca plaza
③ Outdoor learning amphitheater
④ Native herbs

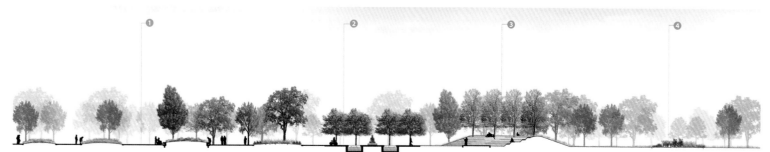

Elevation plan 3

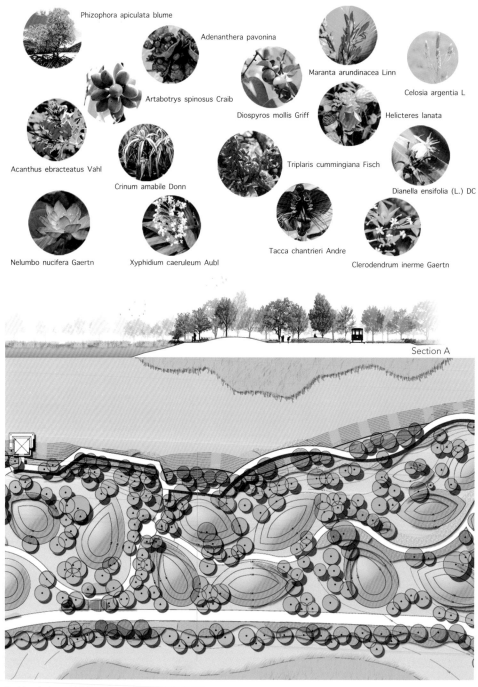

Phizophora apiculata blume

Adenanthera pavonina

Artabotrys spinosus Craib

Maranta arundinacea Linn

Celosia argentia L

Diospyros mollis Griff

Helicteres lanata

Acanthus ebracteatus Vahl

Crinum amabile Donn

Triplaris cummingiana Fisch

Dianella ensifolia (L.) DC

Nelumbo nucifera Gaertn

Xyphidium caeruleum Aubl

Tacca chantrieri Andre

Clerodendrum inerme Gaertn

Section A

Highland plant exhibit

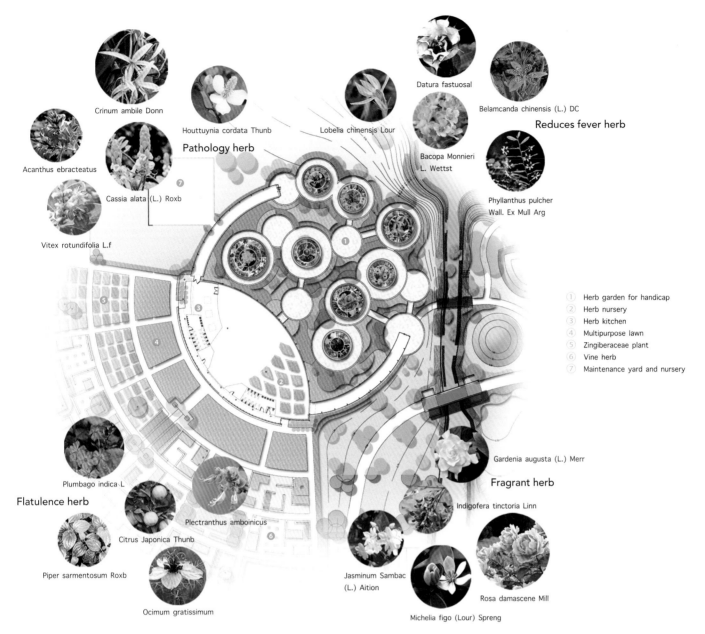

Crinum ambile Donn

Acanthus ebracteatus

Cassia alata (L.) Roxb

Houttuynia cordata Thunb

Vitex rotundifolia L.f

Pathology herb

Lobelia chinensis Lour

Datura fastuosal

Belamcanda chinensis (L.) DC

Reduces fever herb

Bacopa Monnieri
L. Wettst

Phyllanthus pulcher
Wall. Ex Mull Arg

① Herb garden for handicap
② Herb nursery
③ Herb kitchen
④ Multipurpose lawn
⑤ Zingiberaceae plant
⑥ Vine herb
⑦ Maintenance yard and nursery

Gardenia augusta (L.) Merr

Fragrant herb

Indigofera tinctoria Linn

Plumbago indica L

Flatulence herb

Citrus Japonica Thunb

Piper sarmentosum Roxb

Plectranthus amboinicus

Ocimum gratissimum

Jasminum Sambac
(L.) Aition

Michelia figo (Lour) Spreng

Rosa damascene Mill

Exhibition area for Handicap

1. Rest area and water access to natural habitat
2. Views in herb park

1. Existing dormitory was modified and utilized as herbarium, seminar room, and management office
2. Observation deck at Sala overlook bird sanctuary in the wetlands
3. Variety of species of plants in raised planter allow easy access to touch, feel, and smell plants
4. Climber zone
5. Boardwalk and bridge at water-plants exhibition zone

① Wetlands and sanctuary
② Boardwalk
③ Herb park

Elevation plan 4

7 | Low-maintenance Technology

Lowering demand for maintenance of landscaping is another technical approach to reduce energy consumption, for example, using low-maintenance materials and indigenous plants. Low-maintenance landscaping has the following major characteristics:

- low workmanship, low-energy consumption, and low loss
- highly public
- easy to clean, maintain, and rebuild

Low-maintenance design of landscaping should not be applied during the last stages of the project, but instead should be adopted in the early process of design, construction, and operation of the whole project.

Overall design of low-maintenance landscaping

To lower maintenance demand for landscaping, we have to begin with the overall landscaping design. An excellent overall layout can improve self-maintenance capabilities of building and expanding of landscape.

Keep in mind of the characters of a reasonable layout

We shall make predictions of crowd flow in the landscaping site as well as the main distribution points of crowds. In this way, we can learn about the site's capacity, facilities, and demands on the environment so as to prevent providing insufficient or unnecessary facilities. When the facilities are insufficient and the crowd flow is too heavy, the vegetation will be destroyed, the environment polluted, and the landscape damaged. If the facilities are excessive and the crowd flow is light, then the maintenance of landscape will be neglected and it is a waste of resources.

Researching activity space and movement lines

Researching the activity space and movement lines in landscaping can help make choices to keep appropriate private space and eliminate dead space; thus neglected corners that are insufficiently maintained can be reduced.

Park Killesberg: Paths in green

Pay attention to treatment of terrain

Sloping sites can create some distinctive landscaping. However, if they are not well designed, the maintenance in later stages will be expensive. For example, when treating a sloping site, we need to prevent the heavy erosion effect of rainwater, otherwise it will wither the plants and cause loss of water and soil. The height of a sloping site shall also be appropriate and the construction shall be properly carried out, otherwise, it will cause cracks and unevenness in the ground due to sedimentation. It may also cause problems in later stage maintenance.

Hard landscaping design

For hard landscaping, the maintenance work primarily includes cleaning, repairing, updating, and removing. Therefore, the design shall take into consideration cost of materials, workmanship, time, and craftsmanship.

Selection of materials for hard landscaping

Use local materials as much as possible to reduce costs of transportation and purchasing as well as time required for maintenance. Choose replaceable materials and dimensions for easier maintaining and repairing. The reliability of materials is another aspect deserving much attention. The durability of stones, stainless steel, and wood is good, while that of glass, gravel, plain carbon steel, and concrete is poor. The anti-pollution capability of materials could also affect the maintenance required; therefore, select materials with stronger anti-pollution capabilities such as polished stones, rubble, and metal. Moreover, the anti-pollution capability of variegated and dark color materials are better than light color ones.

Treatment method of hard landscaping

As long as the landscaping is not affected, the direction of the pavement should be perpendicular or parallel to major edges as much as possible so as to reduce the need for cutting materials. Increase flexible pavement in landscape, especially in landscaping areas with relatively low requirements for flatness, such as footpaths in parks. Try to avoid designs that will easily be subject to damage, such as exposed acute angles or splicing of acute angles.

Design of plants

The design of landscaping plants mainly refers to selection and arrangement of plants. To design landscaping plants with low maintenance requirements, priority should be given to indigenous plants and plants with low curing and management costs. Another good choice for low maintenance is choosing plants with long life, high rates of survival, and high durability of trimming.

Construct more plant communities and try to plant a small amount of grass, appropriate trees, and sufficient shrubs. Plants in communities have stronger vitality and thus their management requirements in later stages are much lower. The reason why we adopt the design of combing trees, shrubs, and grass is that the trees don't need repeated planting and curing, and have low-maintenance costs compared with grass and flowering plants.

A design with low maintenance doesn't aim at providing a technical mean, but a design idea for low maintenance. From the beginning, the design shall be optimized. The designers shall try to provide a long-lasting design scheme for constructing landscape with low-energy consumption and offer a much more energy-saving and endurable landscaping plan.

Jiading Central Park

At the outset, the district's master plan failed to comprehensively understand the impact of cross-traffic on the public green space. In a critical first move, the design team intervened to minimize fragmentation, reducing the number of roadways crossing the park, and constructing pedestrian overpasses or underpasses where roads remained—critically preserving a holistic park experience for wildlife and pedestrians alike.

Sasaki's design concept for the park, 'Dancing in the Woods,' is based on a contemporary interpretation of traditional Chinese painting, calligraphy, and dance. Four major paths in the park interweave and interact with a variety of park elements in a choreographed composition, twisting and turning along the space and landforms. Spatial configurations within the park embrace dichotomies of form and purpose: openness and privacy, monumental and intimate, active and quiet, urban and pastoral, straight and curvilinear, elevated and recessed.

With a strong foundational understanding of the project context and an articulated design vision, the team embarked on a sustainability-driven design that produced outstanding change for the area. This strong commitment to supporting the ecological system and a people-oriented spirit manifests in sustainable design details, including accessibility on all pathways, restored wetlands, new woodlands, native plantings that bolster the local environment, a stormwater management system, limited artificial lighting, and efficient reuse of existing materials and on-site structures.

As a result of an interdisciplinary approach, inspired vision, and meaningful sustainable design, Jiading Park has transformed the area. Restoring wetland and woodland has drastically improved water and air quality and biodiversity; rainwater harvesting has decreased potable water demand by 3.3 million gallons annually; reuse of materials such as asphalt and salvaged roof tiles have reduced emissions and lowered construction costs.

Today's park features clear water and fishermen where dirty canals and algae blooms once proliferated. Birds circle the skies and float on the canal. People of all ages take to the sports fields and wander the paths. The green corridor is the heart of the New City and has quickly become a new signal of vitality for the region.

Location |
Shanghai, China
Completion date |
2013
Site area |
173 acres (70 hectares)
Landscape design |
Sasaki
Client |
Shanghai Jiading New City Development
Company
Photography |
Sasaki Associates, Qianxi Zhang, Xiaotao Gao

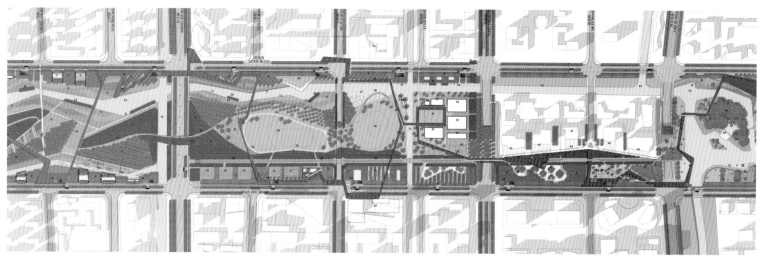

Sustainable features:
• habitat restoration
• stormwater management
• energy efficiency
• water-quality improvements
• native planting material

1. The park was designed not only to foster development, but also to create spaces for people to enjoy the native Shanghai landscape
2. More than 2300 existing trees were preserved and 12,284 new trees were planted, allowing the underutilized site to be transformed into a diverse woodland community

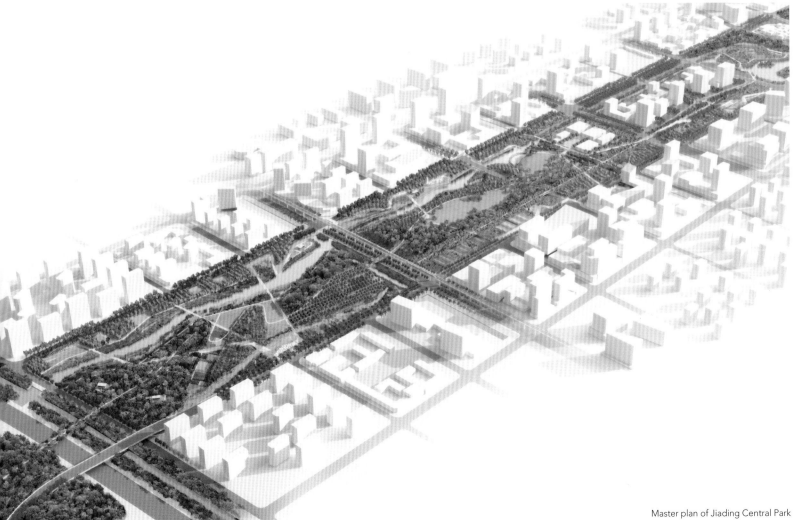

Master plan of Jiading Central Park

1. Jiading Central Park's robust wetland system restores the native ecology of the region and engages visitors in all seasons
2. The park's meadows and understory plantings were an integral part of restoring forest structure, and allow the juxtaposition of openness and intimacy to coexist

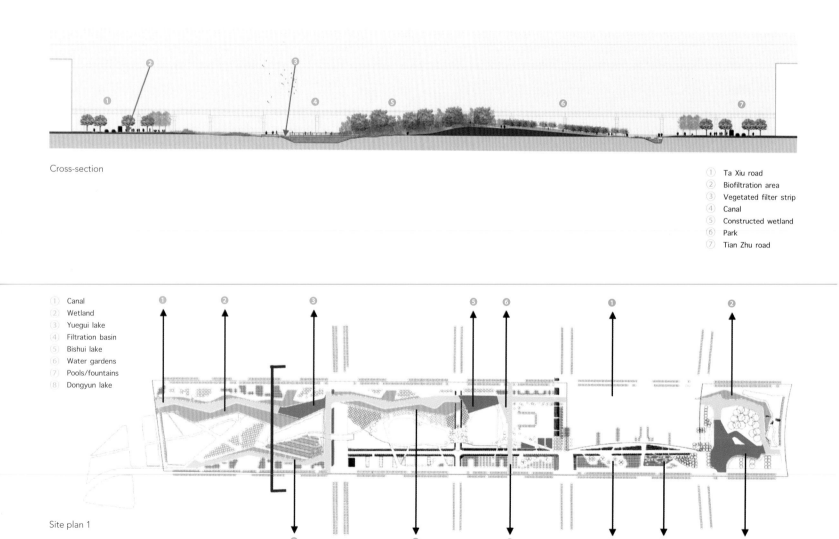

Cross-section

① Ta Xiu road
② Biofiltration area
③ Vegetated filter strip
④ Canal
⑤ Constructed wetland
⑥ Park
⑦ Tian Zhu road

① Canal
② Wetland
③ Yuegui lake
④ Filtration basin
⑤ Bishui lake
⑥ Water gardens
⑦ Pools/fountains
⑧ Dongyun lake

Site plan 1

1|2

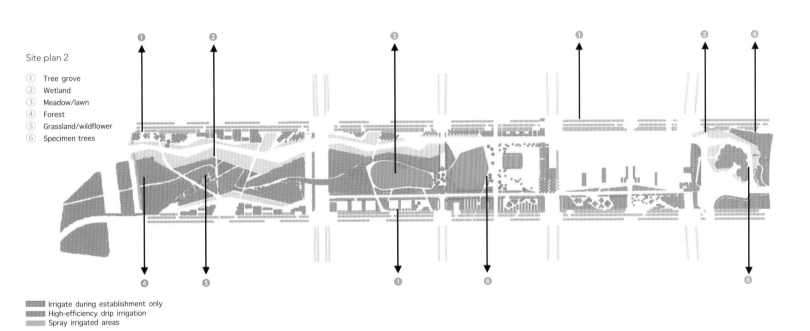

Site plan 2

① Tree grove
② Wetland
③ Meadow/lawn
④ Forest
⑤ Grassland/wildflower
⑥ Specimen trees

▓ Irrigate during establishment only
▓ High-efficiency drip irrigation
▓ Spray irrigated areas

Water cycle

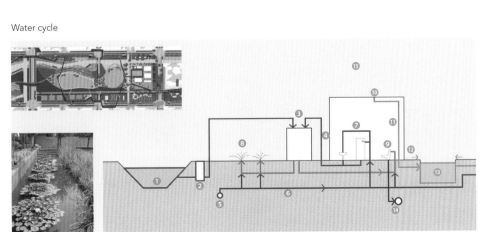

① Canal
② Pump
③ Water filtration and disinfection system (living machine)
④ Greywater
⑤ Supplemental water from potable source
⑥ Potable water
⑦ Sink shower
⑧ Irrigation
⑨ Toilet
⑩ Roof drain
⑪ Rainwater
⑫ Runoff
⑬ Water garden
⑭ Sanitary sewer
⑮ Cultural/interpretative center

Park Killesberg

The overall design premise was to create a pioneering concept for the extension of the park that combines ecology with economy, and allows a new urban environment, different from the usual methods of local authorities. After numerous design studies exploring separate characteristics for the different parts of the green network, the design evolved to achieve a seamless combination of the individual spaces and a cohesive design language for the entire space, thereby maximizing the effectiveness of the complete 'green U.'

Two themes that characterize Killesberg were the starting point for the design: a soft, near-natural landscape, and artificial quarries as hard topographies. The hard forms of typical quarry topography slowly change over time, morphing from sharply broken materials into a softer landscape of green regrowth. This process of change has been recreated at Park Killesberg by bringing vast quantities of soil into the former quarry areas and exhibition grounds, simulating the long natural process of smoothing out irregularities by creating a new topography of lawn 'cushions' between path systems. The underlying theme of the design is based on skewing the perception of human scale and reinterpreting familiar perspectives by raising the topography to eye height and setting up a sunken path network between. The skillful illusion of the new topography intensifies the feeling of being completely absorbed in the landscape, and generates a surprisingly playful experience for the park user—a new sensation. The layout of paths is inspired by the quarries' irregularities, as well as by the gentle winding pattern taken as one climbs the ascent on either side of the street that bisects the park.

The concept of sustainable and ecological development is an underlying theme. Rainwater from the roofs of the new development is collected in an underground cistern from where it is piped to a new lake and returned to the water cycle. With their individual microclimatic conditions, the park's meadow cushions are biotopes for various types of flora and fauna. The meadow grasses require mowing only twice a year, considerably reducing ongoing maintenance costs. The landscape of the Park Killesberg extension interconnects with the adjacent residential area, whose detached houses open directly onto the park, as well as forming a direct connection to the center of the new district.

Location |
Stuttgart, Germany
Completion date |
2012
Site area |
24.7 acres (10 hectares)
Landscape design |
Rainer Schmidt Landschaftsarchitekten GmbH
Associate architect |
Pfrommer+Roeder Landschaftsarchitekten
Principal designer |
Professor Rainer Schmidt

Client |
State Capital City Stuttgart
Photography |
Raffaella Sirtoli
Awards |
European Garden Award, 1st prize,
Innovative Contemporary Concept or
Design of a Park or Garden, 2014
RTF-Award, 1st prize, Landscape
Design 'Built', 2014

$\frac{1}{2}\frac{3}{4}5$

Master plan

1–2. Rainwater retention pond, rainwater from the adjacent development is collected in the pond
3. Inclined planes
4. Meadow 'cushions'
5. Paths in green

1. Interconnected networks
2. Overall view

① Polished stainless-steel sheet
② Natural stone wall
③ Bored pile wall
④ Terrace
⑤ Steel balustrade with mesh
⑥ Water level
⑦ Aquatic plants

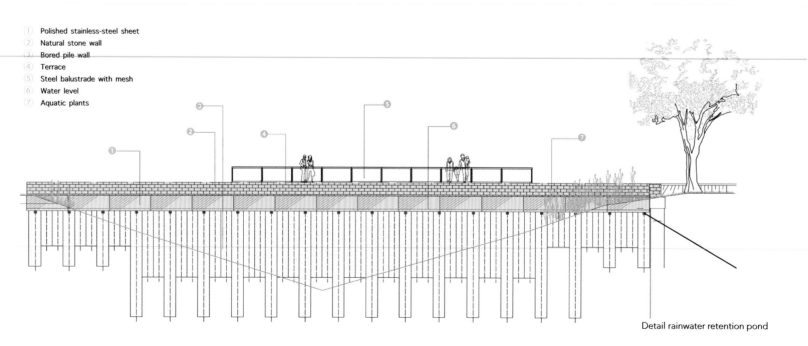

Detail rainwater retention pond

1. Rainwater retention pond, rainwater from the adjacent development is collected in the pond
2. Underground station
3. Path with integrated water management
4-5. Water channel

1 | 3 | 5
2 | 4 |

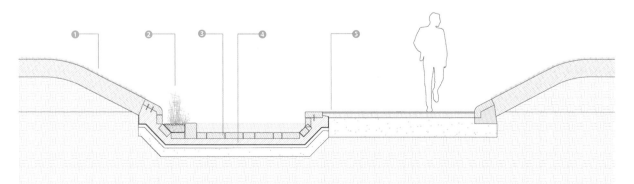

Section

① Grass
② Aquatic plants with substrate
③ Granit stone
④ Concrete
⑤ Pavement

The Center for Sustainable Landscapes

Phipps Conservatory and Botanical Gardens remains at the forefront of the environmental education movement in the United States, and recently completed the construction of the Center for Sustainable Landscapes (CSL), designed to meet four of the world's highest green construction standards. Located on a former brownfield site, the center is a 24,350-square-foot (2250-square-meter) building set within a 2.9-acre (1.17-hectare) landscape that showcases the potential for systems-based design for both research and education. The fully integrated and fully dependent landscape and building generate their own energy, and treat and reuse all water captured on-site.

The steep terrain of the site is made navigable and ADA-compliant through a gently meandering pathway connecting the building's lush green roof to its ground floor. Along this path, visitors may observe more than 150 species of native plants, from open meadows and oak woodlands to water's edge and wetland plantings, which showcase a range of distinct plant communities. These are strategically placed within the topography, reflecting a variety of environmental adaptations. These biodiverse plantings provide food, shelter, and nesting opportunities to endemic wildlife. A 4000-square-foot (372-square-meter) lagoon, fed by conservatory-roof runoff, is populated with native fish and turtles.

The center manages all rainfall and treats all sanitary waste on-site. The center can manage an every-10-year storm event within the site boundaries (3.3 inches [8.4 centimeters] of rain in 24 hours) using soil and vegetation-based systems, including green roofs, rain gardens, bioswales, the lagoon, pervious asphalt, and high-performance native landscapes. No potable water was used for irrigation after the landscape's establishment period. The center also harvests runoff from half an acre (2000 square meters) of rooftop from adjacent buildings outside the site boundary. The harvested water is reused to offset the daily irrigation demand in Phipps's conservatory spaces, significantly reducing the campus's need for municipal water and the energy required to treat and deliver it to Phipps.

The center reveals the potential beauty of renewable-energy technologies, conservation strategies, water-treatment systems, native plants, and sustainable landscaping to a broad audience, including many who are engaging with these topics for the first time.

Location |
Pittsburgh, Pennsylvania, United States
Completion date |
2013
Site area |
2.9 acres (1.17 hectares)
Landscape design |
Andropogon Associates Ltd
Client |
Phipps Conservatory and Botanical Gardens

Photography |
Andropogon Associates, Ltd and Paul G Wiegman
Photography
Awards/Certification |
Four-Star Certified Pilot Project, Sustainable
SITES Initiative, 2014

Living Building Challenge certification, 2015

WELL Certification, measuring human wellness
in the built environment, 2014

LEED Platinum, US Green Building Council, 2014

Rendered concept aerial view

Andropogon JRC 09

1. The core function of the CSL is to increase public awareness of the interconnection between the natural and built environments and the efficacy and synergy of integrated, sustainable building and landscape systems

Site-performance-based landscape-planting design

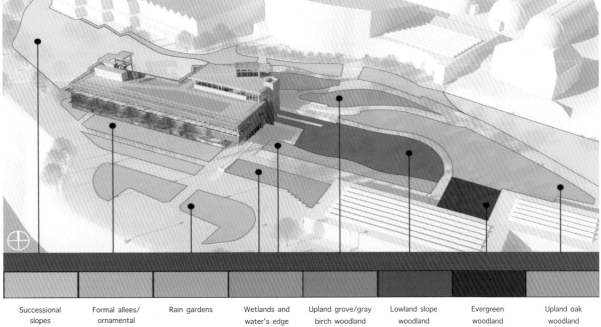

| Successional slopes | Formal allees/ ornamental | Rain gardens | Wetlands and water's edge | Upland grove/gray birch woodland | Lowland slope woodland | Evergreen woodland | Upland oak woodland |

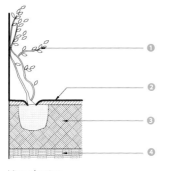

Vine planting

1. Vine
2. Mulch: 2 inch (5.1 centimeter) settled depth, keep away from stems
3. Planting soil
4. Prepared subgrade

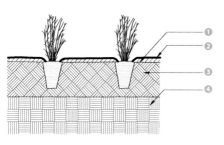

Herbaceous planting

1. Finish grade,
2. Mulch: 3 inch (7.6 centimeter) settled depth, keep away from stems
3. Planting soil
4. Prepared subgrade

Lagoon planting

1. Lagoon planting medium, size C
2. Lagoon planting medium, size L
3. Lagoon rootball soil mix
4. Burlap fabric pocket, open at top
5. Perforated drain pipe

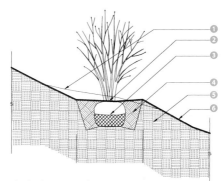

Shrub planting on slope

1. Exist grade
2. Top of root ball set at finish grade
3. Twine, rope, burlap and wire removed from top half of root ball
   (remove non-biodegradable rope and burlap from entire root ball)
4. Backfill planting soil
5. Prepared planting soil
6. Finish grade

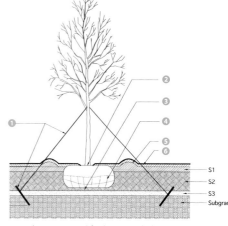

Tree planting typical for lawns and planting beds

1. Stake and staking wire
2. Top of rootball (trunk flare) set at or 1 inch (2.5 centimeters) max. Above finish grade (with trunk flare visible)
3. Pedestal of S2 compacted to 95 percent standard proctor
4. Twine, rope, burlap and wire removed from top half of roof ball
   (removed non-biodegradable rope and burlap from entire root ball)
5. Finish grade
6. Mulch: 2 inch (5.1 centimeter) settled depth, keep away from trunk

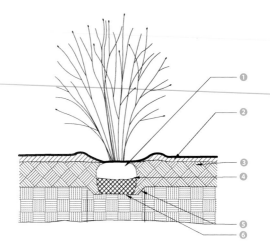

Typical shrub planting

1. Top of root ball set at finish Grade
2. Mulch: 3 inch (7.6 centimeter) settled depth, keep away from stems
3. Planting soil
4. Twine, rope, burlap and wire removed from top half of root ball
   (remove non-biodegradable rope and burlap from entire root ball)
5. 1:1 slope
6. Root ball set on subgrade or tamped soil mound

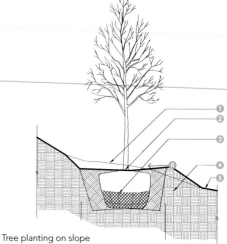

Tree planting on slope

1. Exist grade
2. Top of rootball (trunk flare) set at or 1 inch (2.5 centimeters) max, above finish grade (with trunk flare visible)
3. Twine, rope , burlap and wire removed from top half of root ball.
   (remove non-biodegradable rope and burlap from entire root ball)
4. Prepared planting soil
5. Finish grade
6. Pitch

1–2. A visitor to the CSL can learn firsthand about ecosystem services, the beauty and benefits of native plant habitats, green infrastructure and its role in improving local water quality, and also appreciate the biodiversity that the site is designed to sustain and protect

A. Stormwater capture
B. Green roof system
C. Divert stormwater capture
D. Water storage cistern
E. Lagoon: stormwater storage
F. Rain garden: lagoon overflow

G. Subsurface stormwater storage
H. Pervious asphalt
I. Constructed wetland
J. Greywater sanitary sand filters
K. Subsurface sanitary sand filters
L. UV polishing greywater

The CSL manages a 10-year storm event, including a half-acre (2000 square meters) of rooftop runoff from adjacent buildings, within the site boundaries through soil- and vegetation-based systems. Collected rainwater, rather than potable water, was used during landscape establishment

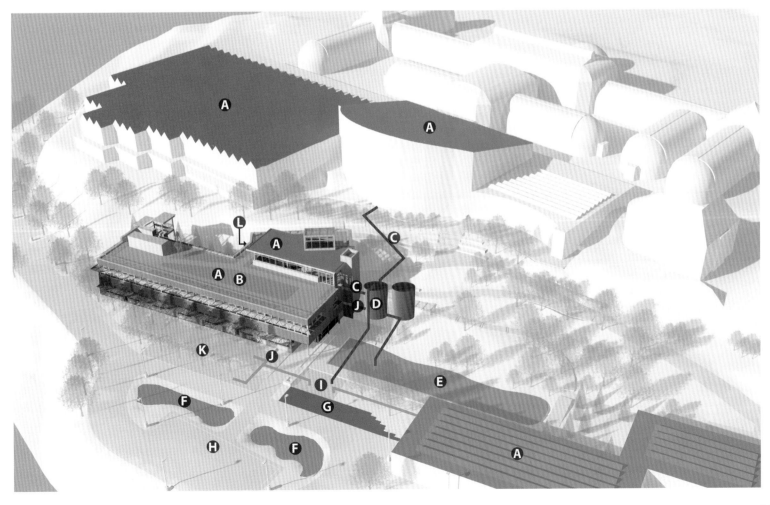

1. Designed to invite public exploration and inquiry, the CSL is uniquely positioned to showcase restorative landscape strategies and ecologically based water treatment systems that use indigenous plant communities as a solution to relieve the aging, urban infrastructure
2. A series of waterfalls provides a tranquil setting and encourages visitors and birds to interact with the water, while continuously oxygenating the rainwater runoff before it returns to the lagoon

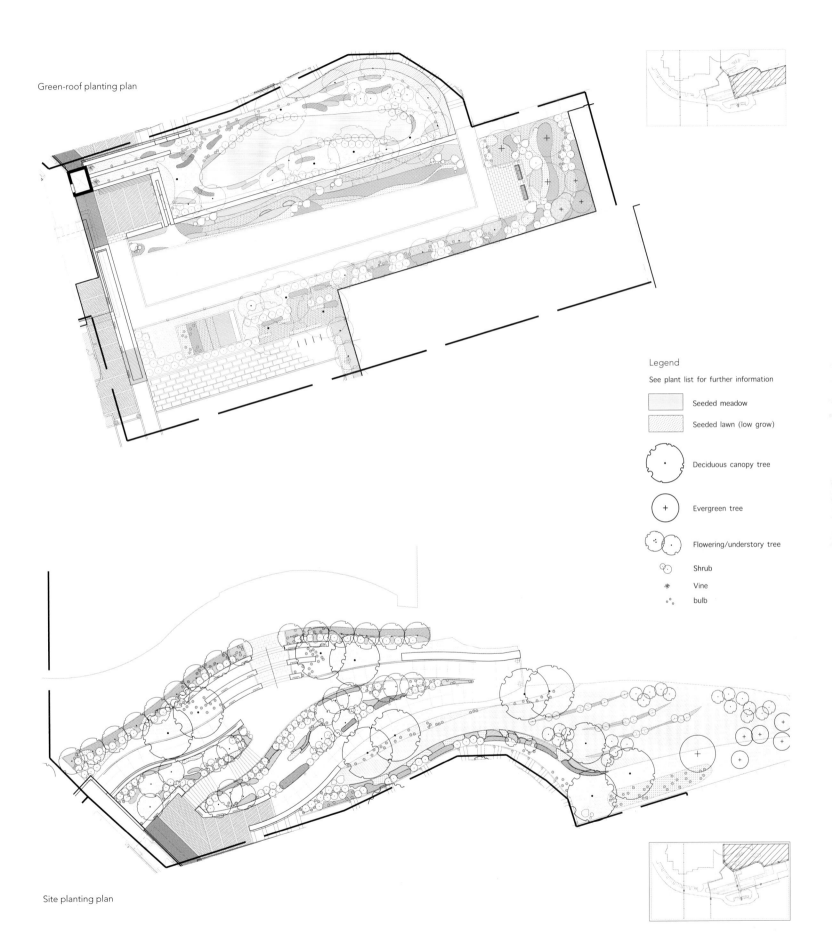

Green-roof planting plan

Legend

See plant list for further information

Seeded meadow

Seeded lawn (low grow)

Deciduous canopy tree

Evergreen tree

Flowering/understory tree

Shrub

Vine

bulb

Site planting plan

223

Coyoacán Corporate Campus Landscape

Located in one of Mexico City's oldest neighborhoods, Coyoacán 1622 stands out as a different approach in corporate buildings in Mexico. Instead of creating a high-rise, the project develops horizontally, taking advantage of the excellent local weather as well as the particularly low scale of the constructions near it. The exterior design takes a major role in becoming the 'transition' that 'glues' one building to the other. The project involved the renovation of an old pharmaceutical laboratory complex to turn it into an office 'campus' park. One of the biggest concerns for the client was that the landscape really integrated the workspace with the exterior, giving the option to also use it as a possible working space for informal meetings or presentations. Four main buildings with different scales and geometry form the complex.

The main concept for the landscape and hardscape design was to depict the integration between inside and out, making the illusion that the plants and trees already existed and that the project was built around it. By Mexican standards, it is considered a pioneer project, where the building scale is more human and the open spaces are designed to increase the users' quality of life. The project is shaped by architectural elements such as 'folded' wooden decks, communication ramps, and green areas at different levels.

All these elements are designed with the intention of providing flexibility, without 'blocking' the visuals, and giving depth to the exteriors, integrating the entire area.

Sustainability was also a major concern, using low-maintenance and long-lasting materials as well as adapted and endemic vegetation. Black volcanic granite was used on the walls and floors with different textures; composite wood (60 percent bamboo, 40 percent non-toxic resin) was used for the wooden decks, and thicker steel plates to conform planters and benches. The landscape design is made of 1.79 acres (7244 square meters), of which 0.81 acres (3278 square meters) are green areas, 0.22 acres (89 square meters) are terraces of wooden decks, and the remainder is given to corridors and the main entrance.

Location |
South Mexico City, Mexico
Completion date |
2013
Site area |
1.79 acres (7244 square meters)
Landscape design |
DLC Architects (María Guadalupe Domínguez
Landa, Rafael López Corona) + Colonnier y
Asociados (Jean Michel Colonnier)

Collaborators |
Mónica Muñóz González, José Agustín
Hernández Cruz
Client |
Colonnier y Asociados / MF Farca
Photography |
DLC Architects

1. Motor lobby plaza view
2. Main access plaza and motor lobby plaza aerial view
3. Main access plaza view.

1 | 2
3

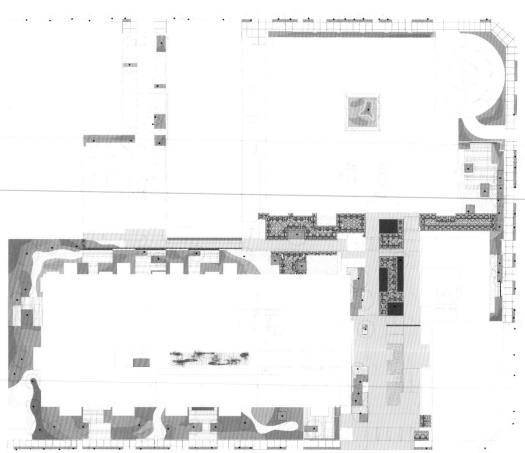

Site plan

1 | 2 | 3

1. Main access plaza and motor lobby plaza aerial view
2. Main access plaza view.
3. Motor lobby water feature and main access plaza aerial view

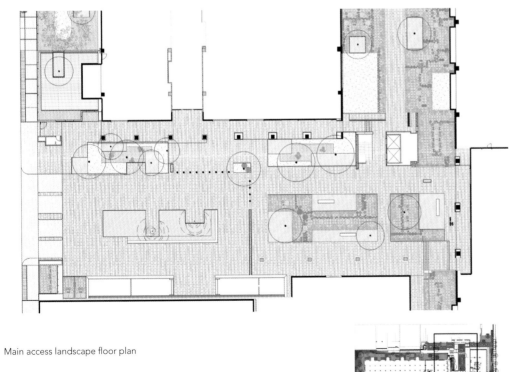

Main access landscape floor plan

N

1. Front yard patios and wooden decks aerial view
2–4. Front patios render aerial view

1	2
	3
	4

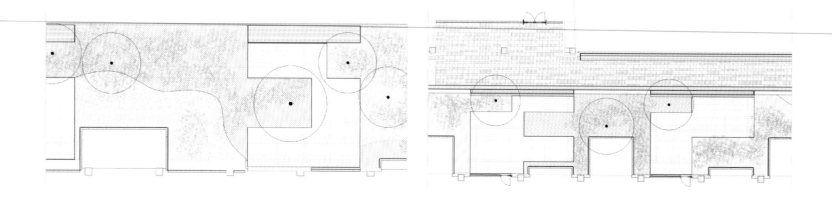

Backyard landscape floor plan

Building yard landscape floor plan

1. Backyard patios and corridor view
2–3. Main entrance building view
4. Corridor and ramp to building view

$\frac{1}{2\mid3}\Big|4$

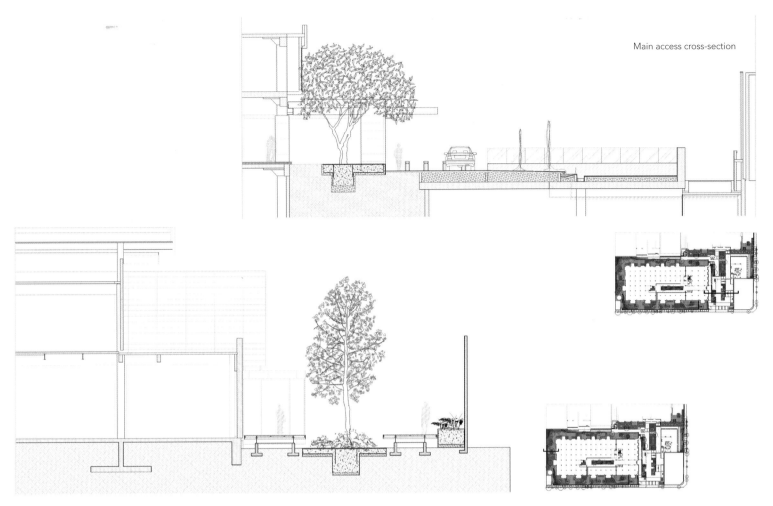

Main access cross-section

Backyard cross-section

Botanic Greenhouse

The new tropical conservatory at the Botanical Gardens in Aarhus is like a drop of dew in its green surroundings. Sustainable design, new materials and advanced computer technology went into the creation of the hothouse's organic form.

The snail-shaped hothouse in the Botanic Gardens is a national icon in hothouse architecture. It was designed in 1969 by C.F. Møller Architects, and is well adapted to its surroundings. Accordingly, it was important to bear the existing architectural values in mind when designing a new hothouse to replace the former palm house which had been literally outgrown.

The organic form and the large volume, in which the public can go exploring among the treetops, present botany and a journey through the different climate zones in a way that makes the new hothouse in Aarhus an attraction in a pan-European class in hothouse architecture.

An assortment of tropical plants, trees and flowers fills the interior of the greenhouses transparent dome set on an oval base. A pond is located at the centre of the space, while an elevated platform allows visitors to climb up above the treetops.

The design of the new hothouse is based on energy-conserving design solutions and on knowledge of materials, indoor climate, and technology.

Using advanced calculations, the architects and engineers have optimised their way to the building's structure, ensuring that its form and energy consumption interact in the best possible manner and make optimal use of sunlight. The domed shape and the building's orientation in relation to the points of the compass have been chosen because this precise format gives the smallest surface area coupled with the largest volume, as well as the best possible sunlight incidence in winter, and the least possible in summer.

The transparent dome is clad with ETFE foil cushions with an interior pneumatic shading system. The support structure consists of 10 steel arches, which fan out around a longitudinal and a transverse axis, creating a net of rectangles of varying sizes. On the south-facing side, the cushions used were made with three layers, two of which were printed. Through changes in pressure, the relative positions of these printed foils can be adjusted. This can reduce or increase, as desired, the translucence of the cushions, changing the light and heat input of the building.

The total project also includes a comprehensive restoration of the old hothouse, in which the palm house becomes a new botanical knowledge centre aimed at the general public, at the same time as the complex is extended with the new tropical hothouse.

The project unites architecture, engineering and landscape architecture so closely that disciplines overlap and become inseparable: in a hothouse, landscape architecture also becomes interior design. The hothouse integrates a natural level difference of 9.8 feet (3 meters) via interior terracing, including rice plants, and sinuous paths around an interior pond landscape with Victoria water lilies and mangroves.

Location |
Botanical Gardens, Aarhus, Denmark
Completion date |
2013
Site area |
35,521 square feet (3300 square meters)
Architect |
C.F. Møller Architects
Landscape design |
C.F. Møller Landscape
Client |
Aarhus University and Danish University &
Property Agency

Engineering |
Steel load-bearing structures: Søren Jensen A/S
Foil cushion planning: formTL GmbH
Photography |
Frans Borgman, Julian Weyer, Quintin Lake
Prizes |
2016: Special Mention in the Architizer A+
Awards Architecture + Engineering category.
2015: Civic Trust Award - Regional Finalist
2014 Aarhus Municipality Architecture Award
2009 1.prize in architectural competition

The double curved base originates from the existing greenhouses, meanders with the surrounding landscape topography, forms the base of the new tropical hothouse, and becomes a retaining wall that encloses the court for storage and containers in one sweeping movement.

A new courtyard, between the new and original Palm Houses used for outdoor seating and dining, is paved with in-situ cast concrete in a triangular pattern so that the surface appears directionless. The triangular planting beds are planted with single species, in contrast to the diversity of the botanical collection.

Structural diagram

ETFE-cushion

East–west tubular profile

North–south tubular profile

Diagonal cables

Plinth

East elevation

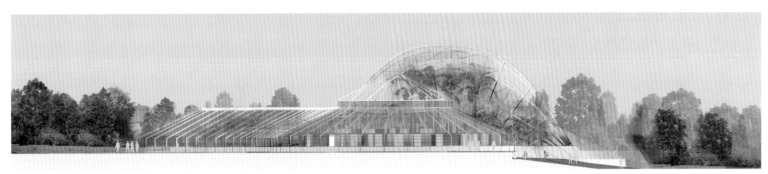

North elevation

West elevation

South elevation

1. The double curved base originates from the existing greenhouses and forms the base of the new tropical hothouse
2. The transparent dome appears light from the surrounding botanical gardens

1. The interplay between the old and new structure has been an essential focal point
2. A new building inserted into the existing hothouse provides space for exhibitions and research

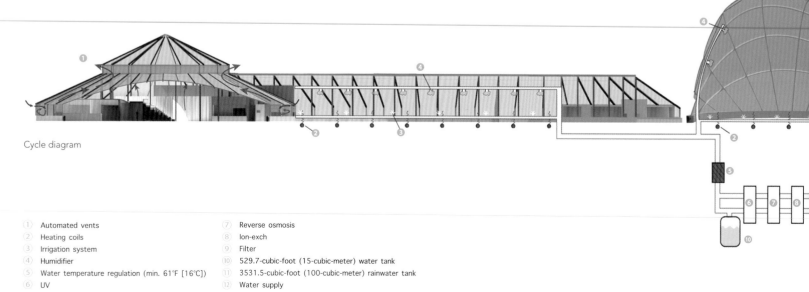

Cycle diagram

①	Automated vents	⑦	Reverse osmosis
②	Heating coils	⑧	Ion-exch
③	Irrigation system	⑨	Filter
④	Humidifier	⑩	529.7-cubic-foot (15-cubic-meter) water tank
⑤	Water temperature regulation (min. 61°F [16°C])	⑪	3531.5-cubic-foot (100-cubic-meter) rainwater tank
⑥	UV	⑫	Water supply

1|2

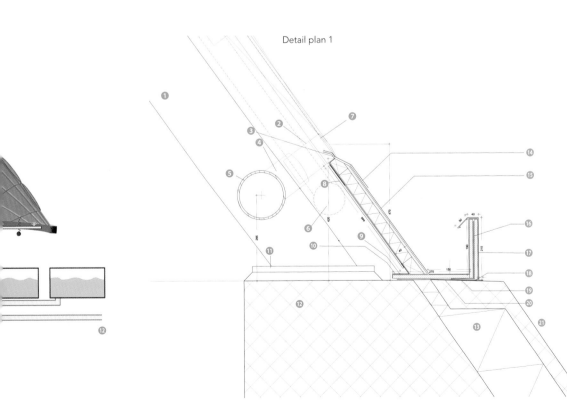

Detail plan 1

① Painted steel arch
② Stainless steel L-section supporting ETFE-mounting
③ Inner sealing membrane glued to roofing felt
④ Welded steel fin
⑤ Painted steel section
⑥ Galvanized air duct for ETFE-cushions
⑦ Aluminium ETFE-mounting section
⑧ Aluminium foil under sealing membrane
⑨ Aluminium foil glued to plywood
⑩ Zinc flashing
⑪ Steel footplate for arch support
⑫ Concrete base
⑬ Insulation
⑭ Sealing foil glued over gutter sealant
⑮ Gutter:
    Roofing foil
    0.4 inches (9 millimeters) Marine plywood
    1.6 inches (40 millimeters) insulation
    Aluminium foil
    0.2 inches (4 millimeters) plastic interlayer
⑯ 0.5 inches (12 millimeters) Marine plywood Steel L-section
    0.5 inches (12 millimeters) Marine plywood Sealant foil
⑰ 0.08 inches (2 milimeters) anodized aluminium ashing
    screwed mounted on plywood and concrete
⑱ EPDM sel
⑲ Roofing felt interlayer
⑳ Inclined top of base, ca. 3 degrees
㉑ Rendered concrete base

239

1–3. The original palm house has become a new botanical knowledge centre aimed at the general public, with a café and seating steps used by school classes etc.

Detail plan 2

① Internal sunscreen
② Automated vents
③ Heating coils
④ Convector

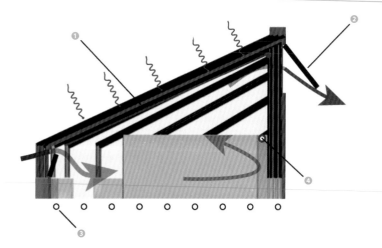

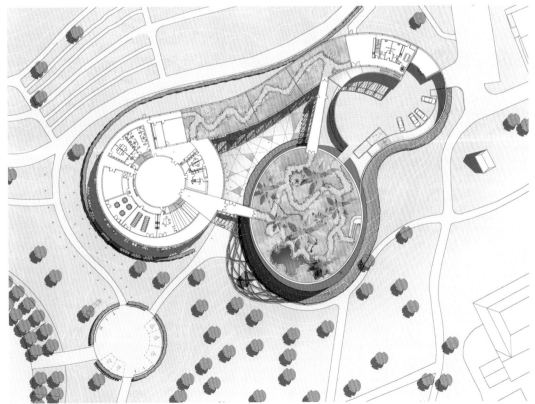

Ground-floor plan

1. The public can go exploring among the treetops via a tall timber platform inside the dome
2. Lush plantings in the greenhouse
3. The hothouse integrates a natural level difference of 9.8 feet (3 meters) via interior terracing and sinuous paths around an interior pond landscape with Victoria water lilies and mangroves
4. The shape of the dome gives the smallest surface area coupled with the largest volume, as well as the best possible sunlight incidence in winter, and the least possible in summer

Index

Rainer Schmidt Landschaftsarchitekten GmbH
P208
Website: www.rainerschmidt.com
Telephone: +49 892025350
Email: info@rainerschmidt.com

Rehwaldt LA
P26
Website: www.rehwaldt.de
Telephone: +49 351 811 96921
Email: ulrike.zaenker@rehwaldt.de

Sasaki
PP74, 202
Website: www.sasaki.com
Telephone: +16179235325
Email: syang@sasaki.com

SLA
P120
Website: www.sla.dk
Telephone: +45 6080 9394
Email: khp@sla.dk

Snehal Shah with Engineering Design and Research Centre
P62
Website: www.snehalshaharchitect.com
Telephone: +91 7927683001
Email : info@snehalshaharchitect.com

Solution Blue, Inc.
P166
Website: solutionblue.com
Telephone: +1 6512895533
Email: jhink@solutionblue.com

Thorbjörn Andersson with Sweco architects
P188
Website: www.thorbjorn-andersson.com
Telephone: +46 852295236
Email: thorbjorn.andersson@sweco.se

Tony Tradewell
P126
Website: www.bellsouth.net
Telephone: +1 3186235567
Email: ttradewell@bellsouth.net

Van Atta Associates, Inc.
P150
Website: www.va-la.com
Telephone: +1 805 7307444
Email: ellen@va-la.com

Z+T Studio
P80
Web: www.ztsla.com
Telephone: +862162808929802
Email: zhoux@ztsla.com

References

Grau, Dieter, 2015, *Urban Environmental Landscape,* Images Publishing Group, Australia.

Li, Chunlai & Xiaoku Yang, 2011, *Solar and Wind Power Grid Connected Technology,* China Water & Power Press, China.

Li, Jun, 2014, *Water-saving: Automatic and Control Technology,* China Agriculture Press, China.

Li, Jun, 2011, *Soil Improvement,* Zhejiang University Press, China.

Peng, Miaoyan, 2011, *Smart and Art Lighting Engineering,* China Electric Power Press, China.

Tilston, Caroline, 2008, *Low-Maintenance Gardens,* John Wiley, Australia.

Wei, Xiangdong & Yanqi Song, 2005, *Urban Landscape,* China Forestry Press, China.

Wright, Michael, 2015, *Rainwater Park: Stormwater Management and Utilization in Landscape Design,* Images Publishing Group, Australia.

Yang, Hua, 2013, *Hard Landscape Detail Manual,* China Architecture & Building Press, China.

Yang, Sheng & Feng Deng, 2013, *Solar and Wind Power Technology,* Publishing House of Electronics Industry, China.

Zhao, Yansong, Jun Zhang & Hailan Wang, 2010, *Accurate Water-saving Irrigation Technology,* Publishing House of Electronics Industry, China.

Zheng, Lijuan et al. 2015, *Water Utilization and Management Technology,* China Water & Power Press, China.

Published in Australia in 2017 by
The Images Publishing Group Pty Ltd
Shanghai Office
ABN 89 059 734 431
6 Bastow Place, Mulgrave, Victoria 3170, Australia
Tel: +61 3 9561 5544 Fax: +61 3 9561 4860
books@imagespublishing.com
www.imagespublishing.com

Title: Modern Urban Landscapes: Creating Energy-Efficient Designs
Author: Martin Coyle (ed.)
ISBN: 9781864706574

For Catalogue-in-Publication data, please see the National Library of Australia entry

Printed by Everbest Printing Investment Limited., Hong Kong/China